D0420599

THE CYBERNETICS OF PREJUDICES
IN THE PRACTICE OF PSYCHOTHERAPY

Other titles in the

Systemic Thinking and Practice Series

edited by David Campbell & Ros Draper

published and distributed by Karnac Books

Credit Card orders, Tel: 071-584-3303; Fax: 071-823-7743

THE CYBERNETICS
OF PREJUDICES
IN THE PRACTICE
OF PSYCHOTHERAPY

in alphabetical order
Gianfranco Cecchin
Gerry Lane
Wendel A. Ray

Foreword by
Bradford P. Keeney

Systemic Thinking and Practice Series

Series Editors
David Campbell & Ros Draper

London
KARNAC BOOKS

This edition first published in 1994 by
H. Karnac (Books) Ltd.
58 Gloucester Road
London SW7 4QY

Copyright © 1994 by Gianfranco Cecchin, Gerry Lane, and Wendel A. Ray.

The rights of Gianfranco Cecchin, Gerry Lane, and Wendel A. Ray to
be identified as authors of this work have been asserted in accordance
with §§ 77 and 78 of the Copyright Design and Patents Act 1988.

All rights reserved. No part of this publication may be
reproduced, stored in a retrieval system, or transmitted in any form
or by any means, electronic, mechanical, photocopying, recording
or otherwise, without the prior permission of the publisher.

British Library Cataloguing in Publication Data

A CIP catalogue record for this book is available from the British Library.

ISBN: 1 85575 056 2

Printed in Great Britain by BPC Wheatons Ltd, Exeter

1197221 1

Learning Resources
Centre

To
Cesare and Suzanna — Gianfranco Cecchin
Walker and Nancy — Gerry Lane
Rayleen, my life companion — Wendel Ray

OTHER BOOKS BY THE AUTHORS

Paradox and Counterparadox, 1978. Mara Palazzoli, Luigi Boscolo, Gianfranco Cecchin, & Giuliana Prata. New York: Jason Aronson.

Milan Systemic Therapy, 1987. Luigi Boscolo, Gianfranco Cecchin, Lynn Hoffman, & Peggy Penn. New York: Basic Books

Irreverence: A Strategy for Therapists' Survival, 1992. Gianfranco Cecchin, Gerry Lane, & Wendel A. Ray. London: Karnac Books.

Resource Focused Therapy, 1993. Wendel A. Ray & Bradford P. Keeney. London: Karnac Books.

Propagations: 30 Years of M.R.I. Influence, in press. Edited by John H. Weakland & Wendel A. Ray. New York: Haworth Press.

CONTENTS

EDITORS' FOREWORD

As series editors we are very pleased to publish a second book by Cecchin, Lane, and Ray, who are actively charting one of the frontiers of systems thinking: the process by which interaction creates new realities. This book follows naturally from the authors' previous collaboration, *Irreverence: A Strategy for Therapists' Survival*. Whereas the latter frees the therapist from too much conviction to any one idea and advocates taking personal responsibility for putting forth many realities, this new book asks us to go one step further: to examine closely our own ideas—our prejudices—and to observe the way they interact with the prejudices of others. This work is also part of a longer tradition in the field which began with the enquiry into the therapist's own experience—the concepts of transference and countertransference. It is as though this area of thought is being updated and reworked for systemic models of therapy.

This is a challenging book. It challenges a therapist's certainty/ therapeutic pride, but if therapists do not reflect on their own prejudices, they are not modelling open, *exploratory thinking* for their clients, who are then left with their own prejudices lying at the heart of the problem. It also challenges the idea that there is an elite group called "therapists" who know things others don't know.

In this time of politically "correct" thinking, there is a danger that all of us will overlook our own biases in order to say the "correct" thing. While it is important to raise awareness in the larger, political arena, it is also crucial that people are able to have local, personal exchanges in which biases and prejudices are acknowledged as the first step to reaching a new understanding. This book moves boldly in this direction. The authors have described, with the accurate detail that "strikes a chord", some of the prejudices we all carry with us into the therapy room. Then they have gone a step further to trace the way these prejudices interact with those the family bring into the room. We think the identification of this process lies at the heart of systemic thinking; and it clarifies the area that will need to be researched further in order to create "systemic units of observation" to allow the field to share concepts and develop new ideas. We hope this book will be the first of many similar investigations, and we are looking forward to the next contribution from these authors.

David Campbell
Ros Draper

London
January 1994

FOREWORD

The *Cybernetics of Prejudices in the Practice of Psychotherapy* by Cecchin, Lane, and Ray is the enthusiastically awaited off-spring of their classic work on irreverence, *Irreverence: A Strategy for Therapists' Survival*. Here, as in their previous seminal charge, they jar therapists into being more acutely aware of their irreverence, or what they now irreverently call "prejudices".

All therapists revere particular ideas, understandings, structures, metaphors, actions, outcomes, complaints, and styles, among other categories of experience. These revered preferences (or prejudices) constantly seduce the therapist into shaping conversations and the whole of therapy towards the direction the therapist desires. To not come to grips with acknowledging that our desires influence our therapeutic work with others is to dangerously ignore our humanness.

The Cybernetics of Prejudices is actually a call for greater honesty in our profession. It demands we begin by confessing our reverences rather than hiding them. This is a serious challenge to those subscribing to a "narrative" understanding of therapy. Many "narrativists", as the team of Cecchin, Lane, and Ray point out, have urged therapists to close the curtain on one-way observing mirrors. Their rationale is that this helps the therapist move towards being more of an equal partner in co-creating the therapeutic conversation.   Unfortunately, a therapist with a closed mirror is easily tricked into proceeding towards the impossible goal of working without prejudices (or reverences). No such therapist exists, and probably should not be created or even imagined.

The human therapist brings a clearer vision of his or her own reverences to the therapeutic table. This clear-sighted therapist is more concerned with asking how to utilize these reverences in a way that is resourceful to all concerned.

I celebrate the Cecchin, Lane, and Ray announcement that it is safe (and necessary) to re-open the curtain and allow the one-way mirror to again shine light upon therapy. The beacon of the irreverent therapist, however, will always be aimed at illuminating the reverences (prejudices) of the therapists. In this way the therapist may become more *accountable* for her or his participation in the therapeutic drama. The realization of this enlightened accountability might move us towards a more responsible profession.

The narrativists have justly rekindled an interest in therapy as the creation of story. I wish to admit that I am not very interested in grandiose efforts to invent a BIG STORY explaining therapy as story or story-making. Such a production feeds the modernist's addiction to totalizing ideologies. Calling one's theory "post-modern" or expertly claiming to be on the same level of rhetorical participation as clients only obfuscates authors to their own closet worship and reverence of foundationalism (or anti-foundationalism), modernism (including all "post" varieties), and Eurocentric hierarchical posturing of the privileged knower.

The time has come to rip open the curtains and expose the mirror of therapy. In such a room, therapists may become more humbled by encountering, accepting, challenging, and utilizing the limitations they bring with their revered prejudices. The raw therapist abandons overly pious efforts to find or manufacture the Holy Grail of textuality, whether it be posed as a narrative or a meta-narrative. Instead, an irreverent embracing of the truth of absurdity encourages tinkering and playing in the theater of therapy. In other words, the irreverence of *The Cybernetics of Prejudices* frees us from being too serious about anything and possibly everything, including stories and BIG STORIES about stories.

Dare I ask whether Cecchin, Lane, and Ray have become the Three Musketeers of family therapy? Beware to all who exercise pompous authority and one-up-gendership in the field. The blind obedience that public-relations-groomed, big-buck workshop stars crave is going to be plagued by these protectors of irreverence. The swords of these reversers of the irreverent are coming your way. With one swift blow of their sharpened blades, legions of Macy-sized balloons will be deflated, revealing to the whole field that the bigger-than-life-comic-book-like-heroes were only empty bags filled with air.

As readers, let us keep a secret from these three irreverent crusaders. When they leave town we can choose to inflate any empty balloon, theory, idea, or story left in their wake. In this choice arising from our desire, we will remember that they helped teach us to face our prejudices and travel full circle through the mirrored cybernetics of revered irreverences.

Bradford P. Keeney
Professor and Director of Scholarly Studies
University of St. Thomas, St. Paul, Minnesota

THE CYBERNETICS OF PREJUDICES
IN THE PRACTICE OF PSYCHOTHERAPY

[The Grand Inquisitor:] . . . we care for the weak too.
They are sinful and rebellious, but in the end they too
will become obedient. They will marvel at us and look on
us as gods, because we are ready to endure the freedom
which they have found so dreadful and to rule over
them—so awful it will seem to them to be free. But we
shall tell them that we are Thy servants and rule them
in Thy name. We shall deceive them again . . . That
deception will be our suffering, for we shall be forced to
lie.

—Fyodor Dostoyevsky

CHAPTER ONE

Introduction

Even though we, the authors, each have very strong views of how to do therapy effectively, which will be described later, we are no longer trying to seek to capture the "correct" way of doing therapy. This book is not an attempt at inventing a new way of treating clients. There are currently so many therapy models to choose from that we think it important to take a break from trying to create a new model and spend some time considering our position.

Of course, in the end, we anticipate that if one spends time thinking about one's own position and the prejudices that colour it, a natural consequence may be the creation of an idiosyncratic method. We are definitely not proposing that self-reflection become a new model. Perhaps we are proposing that therapists become more playful and aesthetically curious, playmates of novel ideas, liberated from a Stalinist sense of being prohibited from deviating from orthodoxy. We hope to stimulate ourselves to avoid becoming stymied by the dominant culture, including the prevailing therapy models that we helped to create and perpetuate. How can we come out of the limits of our own creations which can unwittingly dupe

1

ourselves and other well-meaning therapists into contributing to the creation of a culture of dunces, unwilling to move beyond self-established limitations?

We believe that acknowledging one's own prejudices is an act of responsibility. When we think about the idea of responsibility we find it is a very easy thing to *say* responsibility, but a very difficult thing to *be* responsible. As Rorty (1991) explains, in many ways the mental health professions have done little to clarify the issue of responsibility:

> The increased ability of the syncretic, ironic, nominalist intellectual to move back and forth between, for example, religious, moral, scientific, literary, philosophical, and psychoanalytical vocabularies without asking the question "And which of these shows us how things really are?—the intellectual's increased ability to treat vocabularies as tools rather than mirrors—is Freud's major legacy. He broke some of the last chains that bind us to the Greek idea that we, or the world, have a nature that, once discovered, will tell us what we should do with ourselves. He made it far more difficult than it was before to ask the question "Which is my true self?" or "What is human nature?" By letting us see that even in the enclave which philosophy has fenced off, there was nothing to be found save traces of accidental encounters, he left us able to tolerate the ambiguities that the religious and philosophical traditions had hoped to eliminate. [p. 158]

Being responsible is very costly, unusual, and extraordinary. The rare leap into responsibility is so uncommon that it may happen only once in a lifetime—Jesus Christ, Einstein, Marx, Freud are examples of major leaps out of the conventional constructions of reality.

One of the earliest mythologies of irreverence towards the dominant wisdom is the story of Eve rebelling against absolute perfection and the responsibility void of the garden of Eden. By taking the first bite from the forbidden fruit she risked entering into the perilous world of responsibility and accountability. These rare instances of originality inevitably become an orthodoxy. Much of the time the creative flash is fear-evoking, eventually to be absorbed and recycled, becoming the irrefutable truth of the moment, to be flattened out into banality. What begins as imaginative renewal of the human spirit soon becomes the prevailing orthodoxy. We consider this a natural phenomenon which remains a mystery.

How is it that humanity seems to fear these instances of creation? How is it that we succumb to the influences of one thing or another—the market, the profession, the client, the socially constructed realities that dictate what one should and must be or do? There are many theories—one is the classical systemic idea of homeostasis: the more things change the more they stay the same. Another is chaos theory—the notion that existence is made up of random acts which humans desperately try to organize into coherent and predictable explanations. Another is religious monotheistic fundamentalism—the idea of one God who organizes a grand scheme which we must accept and trust. For the psychologically minded, there is the idea that insecurity creates addiction to orthodox adherence to a particular prejudice. If we adhere to this view it becomes very difficult, even dangerous, to be irreverent to the prevailing truth. These flashes of generativity become ahistorical orthodoxies, detached from the living narrative of the local communities from which they emerged.

We would like to propose the idea of irreverence as a kind of protection from the power of addiction to anything—ideas, love, helping, food, connection, compassion, heroin, therapy, etc.

There are natural consequences to being overly obedient (addicted) to any of the mandates of the various socially constructed realities. Unwittingly one can become detached from the historical process you are involved in at the moment. It can blind you from seeing different options—more novel ways of experiencing life—dulling your sense of being part of the world you live in. It can destroy art and the aesthetic. Taken to the extreme you have whole cultures, such as Nazi Germany, Communist Russia, contemporary Iraq, etc., where deviation from the correct is deemed extremely hazardous to the survival of the state.

The irreverent position we are proposing is not a new idea. In mediaeval times, the feast of fools, or carnival, was a time during which conventional orthodoxies were transcended much in the same spirit and in the same way that we use irreverence.

The suspension of all hierarchical precedence during carnival time was of particular significance. Rank was especially evident during official feasts; everyone was expected to appear in the full regalia of his calling, rank, and merits and to take the place corresponding to his position. It was a consecration of inequality. On the contrary, all were considered equal during carnival. Here, in the town square, a special form of free and familiar contact reigned among people who were usually divided by the barriers of caste, property, profession, and age. The hierarchical background and the extreme corporative and caste divisions of the medieval social order were exceptionally strong. Therefore, such free, familiar contacts were deeply felt and formed an essential element of the carnival spirit. People were, so to speak, reborn for new, purely human relations. These truly human relations were not only a fruit of imagination or abstract thought; they were experienced. The utopian ideal and the realistic merged in this carnival experience, unique of its kind.

This temporary suspension, both ideal and real, of hierarchical rank created during carnival time a special type of communication impossible in everyday life. This led to the creation of special forms of marketplace speech and gesture, frank and free, permitting no distance between those who came in contact with each other and liberating from norms of etiquette and decency imposed at other times. A special carnivalesque, marketplace style of expression was formed. [Bakhtin, 1965, p. 10]

A historical story comes to mind—the tragic tale of Galileo. A very religious man, Galileo felt a great devotion to the church and the Pope, but could not deny what he had demonstrated as a scientist—that the earth revolved around the sun. This dual loyalty led Galileo to be an irreverent man by making public his scientific knowledge, in spite of his desire not to disobey the church. He was asked by the church to declare his discovery a hypothesis, in order to save his life. But to become irreverent to his discovery was too much for him. He chose to be excommunicated, which ultimately contributed to his death. It is interesting that it is only now, 350 years later, that the church has decided Galileo was not guilty of heresy. The tension that lasted such a long time between the orthodox church and science has probably contributed greatly to the development of science, and conversely to the bolstering of the faith of the true believers which grew stronger by having a magnificent enemy in the sciences with whom to keep the debate alive. We wonder whether the church would have forgiven Galileo earlier if science had become part of the church orthodoxy, possibly inhibiting the irreverent spirit on which science thrives.

This oscillation between orthodoxy and irreverence is part and parcel of the drama of living. Both are part of the fabric of human culture, which is immersed in language. Too much orthodoxy can lead to passivity, totalitarianism, numbing of the creative spirit, and eventually violence. Too much irreverence can lead to terror at the thought of having nothing firm to hold on to, to social disintegration (witness the former state of Yugoslavia), and into addiction to messiahs who are beyond accountability, to violence in its many forms.

One may wonder what this has to do with the practice of psychotherapy. Irreverence, perhaps, suggests the possibility of being responsible rather than becoming the dupe of some rigid proscription from one of the many socially constructed realities.

Responsibility is a very difficult feat, which is why we prefer to use the idea of accountability when we talk about therapy. In part, accountability means being aware of the potential dangers of your own prejudices. It also means you have a duty to have colleagues available, behind the mirror, or available for consultation to help you avoid being unknowingly seduced by the power of your own prejudices. Accountability also involves self-survival: protecting oneself from exploitation by clients, employers, colleagues, or others—exploitation that can take on many forms. Prejudices, accountability, and irreverence will be the topics of this volume.

CHAPTER TWO

A theory of
the cybernetics of prejudices

The American Heritage Dictionary of the English Language provides several definitions for the term prejudice, the second of which fits our use of the term: **Prejudice—** *A preconceived preference or idea. A bias.* To elaborate on this brief definition, we are in agreement with Gadamer that the notion of prejudice is not in and of itself a negative thing (Cecchin, Lane, & Ray, 1991, 1992, 1993). Furthermore, we firmly believe that it is useful for therapists to understand what their prejudices are. According to Gadamer:

> It is not so much our judgements as it is our prejudices that constitute our being. This is a provocative formulation, for I am using it to restore to its rightful place a positive concept of prejudice that was driven out of our linguistic usage by the French and English Enlightenment. It can be shown that the concept of prejudice did not originally have the meaning we have attached to it. Prejudices are not necessarily unjustified and erroneous, so that they inevitably distort the truth. In fact, the historicity of our existence entails that prejudices, in the literal sense of the word, constitute the initial directedness of our whole ability to experi-

ence. Prejudices are biases or our openness to the world. They are simply conditions whereby we experience something—whereby what we encounter says something to us. This formulation certainly does not mean that we are enclosed within a wall of prejudices and only let through the narrow portals those things that can produce a pass saying, "Nothing new will be said here." Instead we welcome just that guest who promises something new to our curiosity. But how do we know the guest whom we admit is one who has something new to say to us? Is not our expectation and our readiness to hear the new also necessarily determined by the old that has already taken possession of us? [1987]

When we talk about prejudices we mean all the sets of fantasies, ideas, accepted historical facts, accepted truths, hunches, biases, notions, hypotheses, models, theories, personal feelings, moods, unrecognized loyalties—in fact, *any* pre-existing thought that contributes to one's view, perceptions of, and actions in a therapeutic encounter. Like Rorty (1989), we believe human prejudices are inevitable and exhibit themselves in language:

> All human beings carry about a set of words which they employ to justify their actions, their beliefs, and their lives. These are the words in which we formulate praise of our friends and contempt for our enemies, our long-term projects, our deepest self-doubts and our highest hopes. They are the words in which we tell, sometimes prospectively and sometimes retrospectively, the story of our lives. I shall call these words a person's "final vocabulary". [p. 73]

We are interested not only in the prejudices of the therapist, but equally in the biases and beliefs of our clients. Therapy occurs in the interplay of the prejudices of therapist and client—a cybernetics of prejudices. Therapy necessarily involves a constant exchange between therapist and client(s) in which the actions and utterances of one are constantly informed, take on meaning, and are shaped by and shape those of the other. The process is cybernetic in that it is outcomes that shape the behaviour of both therapist and client. That is, the meaning of any behaviour is found within the context of the subsequent behaviour it evokes, whether in oneself or others (Ray & Keeney, 1993).

Accepting, for the moment, this as our working definition of the concept of prejudice, we will begin this discussion by looking at some prevalent prejudices, and some of the consequences of these prejudices, within the field of family therapy, brief therapy, psychotherapy, and Western culture.

THE WOUNDED THERAPIST

We noticed an interesting article in the September 9th, 1992, edition of the *New York Times*. The story focused on how the personal history of a therapist affected his or her prejudices and practice. Most therapists described in the article thought they had been abused or neglected by their families during childhood. In adolescence or young adulthood these therapists described how they usually had come across someone who had helped them overcome this "mistreatment" by their parents. The story indicated that many of these individuals then became therapists, going into the field of psychotherapy in order to try to offer clients the same help they had received.

A theme implicit in this caricaturization of the life experiences of therapists is the story of helping. Thus we have what are called the helping professions. Quite often, implicit in this theme of helping is the idea that what people need is warmth, understanding, and, at times, even love. This is an extremely powerful and common prejudice within our culture today, and one that many of us therapists share. How did we get to this absurd position?

The belief that people need warmth and understanding seems to be a peculiar evolution from the time Freud developed psychoanalysis, which involved exploring the unconscious life of people in order for them to gain insight into transference relationships. Prior to Freud's invention of unconscious processes and psychoanalysis, emotional and behaviour disturbances were managed primarily by the church. This recycling of psychoanalysis and Christianity, two extremely powerful traditions, combined with the liberal concepts of equality and co-operation produced, we believe, what we now call the helping professions. This could be an example of how brilliant insights into human nature can be reorganized into an orthodoxy that appears sophisticated but in our opinion seems rather superficial. Common denominators are often superficial.

After having read this *New York Times* article, we began to think about how many of us therapists seem to become caught up in or motivated by a desire to teach people how to attain an ideal:

- how to raise your children correctly as a father
- the correct way to raise your children as a mother
- how parents should talk to each other in front of their children
- how to spend quality time with your children/spouse/pet, etc.
- how to keep the proper distance from in-laws
- how to have quality sex with your spouse
- how to be close without being sexual with your children
- how to have a healthy affair
- how to have a successful divorce without harming your children or your mother
- how to be your own best friend without talking to yourself in public
- how to eat enough while not eating too much
- how to remain in love with the same spouse regardless of physiological time
- how to keep in touch with your inner child and maintain a healthy belief in the future
- etc.

THE MISSIONARY THERAPIST

We asked some of our colleagues what they thought about their own experiences of growing up, only to discover that, although there were those who felt abused as children, a good many others felt that they came from very healthy families with loyal traditions.

The approach of the latter group to therapy seems to involve transmitting what they consider to be the healthy patterns received in their family to other people. They believe that since they did not suffer in childhood, somehow they know what normal is and how a family or individual *should* behave. These therapists seem to have the idea that they owe something to others and that other families want what they have to give, whether they realize it or not. Since their life was so good, they should give something back to these less fortunate others. This form of prejudice is what we like to call the missionary therapist.

EXTREMES OF PREJUDICES

Let us now look at the dangers inherent when therapists become extreme in either of the two prejudices just mentioned. The missionary therapist, for example, can become somewhat of an aristocrat who tends to think he knows what is best for everyone. Many patients or clients are drawn to this kind of certainty. The missionary therapist, or the therapist who is convinced that he or she knows better than the client what healthy is, represents a type of reality testing for clients. In other words, clients have to go to this expert to find out what is real and is not real. A dilemma here, however, is that the clients who have to go to the professional to discover what reality is and what is the best way to live will inevitably feel slightly handicapped, always needing reassurance from a wise professional rather than taking the risk of taking responsibility to live their own lives.

Therapists who engender this kind of relationship with clients tend to present their personal convictions as truth. An escalation can be created in which the therapist becomes somewhat of an elitist. Such therapists frequently write books about what one should do in order to lead a normal life—books that expose the real "reality."

Both the wounded and the missionary therapist prejudices have similar consequences. There is equal danger of the client becoming addicted to the unconditional love from the therapist, in the one case, and to the therapist's authority in the other. Addiction usually becomes enhanced by the subtle but strong negative connotation implicit in these kinds of relationships. In the one case, the client ends up perceiving himself and being treated like a child whose judgement of reality is faulty. In the other, the client is perceived and treated as a someone who has received faulty nurturing and needs a corrective love experience.

Both of these patterns of client–therapist interaction can be described as self-perpetuating, symmetrical escalations. In the first instance the more "needy" the client posture, the more loving/ nurturing the therapist becomes. In the other, the more incompetent the client posture, the more psycho-educative the therapist becomes and vice versa. Like all patterns of this type, no one knows who starts them or how or why they get started. All we know is that these patterns are very common and often end dramatically: addiction to therapy, suicide of the client or the therapist, the therapist moving or changing profession, therapist or client abuse, sex, or sometimes the discovery by either client or therapist of a healthy irreverence towards these absurdly binding reigns of error.

For example, the therapist could suddenly realize how unhelpful he has been for the client and confess his past inefficiency (of course without apologizing or refunding the fee). Or the client could become tired of considering himself a damaged person and set himself free. The last probability is less likely, we think, because the therapist might claim this is to be a successful case thus reinforcing his original prejudices—it takes a lot of emotional strength on the part of the client to allow a therapist working under this kind of prejudice to feel he has been successful. This is one reason why a consultation, in which both therapist and patient can be actively encouraged to deal with an impasset, can be a more effective way of breaking such a therapeutic gridlock.

YET ANOTHER BRIEF AND BIASED HISTORY OF OUR FIELD

During the modern period of psychotherapy, starting with Freud, the field of psychotherapy has attempted to cleanse the therapist of prejudices or pathologies by requiring him or her to undergo personal psychotherapy. This method was based on a premise which implies that therapists must first gain their own mental health by developing thorough insight and knowledge of themselves before being capable of helping clients become more healthy. This unavoidably reinforced the questionable notion that therapists could be judged to be healthy or unhealthy in isolation from their inter-personal contexts, which included the therapeutic relationships with their clients.

After the great revolution of family therapy, led by what has become known as the Palo Alto group, a shift occurred in which the attention was focused on how family members interact with each other through verbal and non-verbal communication. During this first-order cybernetic period, the prejudices the therapist brought into the situation were not considered to be as relevant. Family therapy was a matter of focusing on patterns of interaction within the family and interrupting them, when deemed unhealthy, through manipulation. For example, during the 1950s when the Bateson research group members ran into an impasse in therapy, Haley reports that in supervision Don Jackson would always ask "What did you do to bring about that kind of response from them?" One must remember that, during this period, making the break with psychoanalysis took tremendous courage and radical procedures. Jackson rarely asked questions about what the thera-pist might feel or think about the client. He was only interested in what the therapist did and the client's response to what he did. Jackson's concern with the pragmatics of therapy was very neces-sary in helping to shift away from the psychoanalytic obsession with the intrapsychic and discerning the meaning people attach to experience. This was necessary and important in moving us out of the endless interpretive quagmire.

In more recent years another shift occurred. Attention moved from the Palo Alto group's interest in the pragmatics of communi-cation to an equal curiosity in semantics: the meanings people attach to their experiences and how families (and other social groups) construct meanings or realities. Practitioners from this group (Haley's Strategic Therapy and the MRI Brief Therapy) con-tinue to be interested primarily in how to change people by influ-encing actions of the client (usually an individual). MRI Brief Therapy does this by tracking attempted solutions of the client, reframing the client's story and interrupting attempted solutions; Haley's Strategic Therapy does this by tracking sequences of inter-action and addressing what is seen as an inappropriate hierarchy. Following in the same tradition, de Shazer and Berg's solution-focused approach attends to and expands upon exceptions to the problem.

The early Milan group built upon the cybernetic ideas from the Palo Alto group by making a systemic reframing of the entire family through use of a position of neutrality, hypothesizing, and positive connotation. The emphasis of this work was to develop an understanding of the story of the entire family, not just a single individual. The prejudices of the therapist continued to be considered irrelevant—emphasis was on the story of the family.

The narrative movement (Goolishian and Anderson, Andersen, White, Hoffman, and others) placed even more emphasis on the story of the client to the point of inviting the therapist to become an active listener, inventing the art of how not to do anything that may interrupt the bringing forth of the client's story. The most the therapist could do was to co-create the story through a very skilful dialogue aimed at protecting the client from the therapist's prejudices and interference. The therapist was not to become a colonizer, was not to impose any view on the client. Like many in the field we were very impressed with this orientation. It was attractive because it seemed to represent a position of non-authority and ultimate respect for the imagination of the client and of underplaying the imposition of the therapist's prejudices.

We have to confess that we tried without success to adopt the narrative position. At first we felt awkward and uneasy, because the effort to control our own thoughts and prejudices was not successful. Even at moments when we felt we were being successful in controlling the urge to have a thought, observers were able to point out at least three prejudices implicit in our behaviour in the relationship with the client.

We felt compelled to reconsider our position. Why shouldn't we take seriously the thoughts and prejudices evoked in us in the relationship with the client? The dilemma was how to do this while avoiding falling back into the psychoanalytic paradigm of transference–countertransference, of therapists' psychopathology, and still retain a systemic orientation. A great aid was Bateson's classical idea of levels of abstraction, content, and process. We could organize ourselves to look not at the content of the prejudices of the therapist or client, but rather focus on the relationship between the prejudices of therapist and client which emerges in the context of the therapeutic encounter. In this way we utilize the template of cybernetic description and pattern to examine the relationship between different prejudices and what is created out of this inter-play. We are now at a point where the stories of both the client *and* the therapist become the focus of interest. More will be said about our own clinical prejudices in the next chapter.

Now that we are no longer looking for the truth, or interested in the truthfulness of premises, we have become more interested in the relationship between prejudices. Rather than search for correctness, what is important is to consider how our own prejudices fit, are affected by, and interfere with the hierarchy of prejudices and actions of our clients.

We believe that therapists must be made aware of their own prejudices and how they can affect the prejudices of others (clients, colleagues, institutions, etc.). If therapists can view their models, hypotheses, and techniques as prejudices rather than unquestion-able facts, they are less likely simply to attempt to force these biases on to others. Rather, they are more likely to engage in open dialogue with others about the implications of different biases.

Of course, we believe that some prejudices are more useful than others—but we accept that even these strongly held biases are open to scrutiny and discussion. Even strongly held beliefs—such as that loving children is better than ignoring them, or that co-operation is better than fighting—can be put on the table for examination, if not with the client at least with one's colleagues. We believe that *any* bias or belief worth holding deserves to be scrutinized and open to reconsideration depending upon the context. If a prejudice is isolated from the context within which it makes sense, you stop the conversation: the system (conversation, family, therapy, society) gets stuck. Even the belief that children should always be loved rejects the possibility that, in some instances, ignoring your child can be appropriate. We are not talking about situational ethics. Rather, we want to entertain the idea that context is always a factor that cannot be avoided.

We believe that therapy has come of age. As a profession we can handle the dark side of life by talking about it rather than by avoiding certain subjects and pretending it does not exist. Certainly, even within this statement there is a bias that open discussion is often conducive to resolving problems. One can, at times, assume that the opposite—not encouraging open dialogue between various biases—can be useful. But for our purposes here we stick to the position of openness and are willing to be held accountable for it.

But the situation is even more complicated. Prejudices can be conceptualized in terms of a hierarchy. The interplay between various prejudices present within the same group, within the individuals in the group, within the therapist, between the therapist and his or her colleagues and the institution, and between the therapist and clients has to be taken into consideration. For example, some may value survival above adherence to a strongly held belief that people should not kill one another. Someone may greatly value loyalty to others, but be willing to advocate this belief in the name of protecting his or her own sense of self-respect. Some may value money over love, or love over money; loyalty to one's family of origin over love for your spouse; belief in God and country over self-interest, etc. (See Bateson, 1951, 1972, and Keeney, 1983, for descriptions of methods for mapping hierarchies.)

The personal prejudices of helping, or the desire to impart reality to the client, come from life experiences and can, at times, override the most accepted models of therapy. Therapists who strongly believe in helping seem to have accepted rather uncritically a widely held premise of the Western world: that help is always something good and magnificent. This bias, rooted in the Judeo/Christian tradition, is so much a part of conventional logic that it is taken for granted and, for the most part, unquestioned. It is our contention, shared by many colleagues (Jackson, 1967a; Weakland, Fisch, Watzlawick, & Bodin, 1974; Haley, 1976; de Shazer, 1982) that seeing the client as some poor suffering person, who only needs help and compassion to overcome his or her problems can be disrespectful.

A number of the traditional psychotherapy models were designed to help the therapist protect the family from his own personal prejudices. We recognize the value of clinical models, but we no longer try to prevent ourselves or our trainees from utilizing their personal prejudices. It is our sense that no matter how well

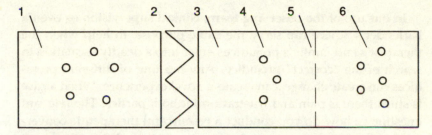

1. Family therapy room
2. One-way mirror
3. Team room
4. Therapy team
5. Invisible boundary separating the team and observing team
6. Observing team

FIGURE 1: *Traditional family therapy setting with an observing team*

versed a person is in a model, or how well supervised he is—regardless of how much personal therapy he may have undergone—his personal biases will always seep in. Not only is this unavoidable, it is not a bad thing—as long as the therapist recognizes that he is accountable for his beliefs and actions and presents them to clients not as fact but as his personal constructions. The art and craft of teaching systemic therapy involves developing innovative ways to help the therapist realize that his ideas are not truth, but prejudices derived from his own experience in living.

Therapy occurs when the prejudices of the family and the therapist interact. The kind of relationship that will emerge also derives from the encounter of the prejudices of the family and therapist. So, from our systemic perspective, it is not the content of the prejudice, but the relationship between the prejudices of the client and therapist that is the heart of the therapy.

The observing team, which has been in practice for a few years and whose task is to observe how the therapeutic team organize their own ideas and interventions, has been of great value in studying the biases of the family, the therapist, the therapy team, and the interaction between them (see Figure 1).

In our use of the observing team, clinical supervision or even a bartender's advice can serve the same purpose: to help when the therapist's and family's prejudices enter into a deadly escalation in search of the "correct" prejudice. Any meeting of different prejudices can create change, can create a novel experience. When a case is stuck there is pain and frustration for both parties. The relevant question is: how do you conduct a resourceful therapeutic conversation in such a way that escalation or symmetrical struggle do not arise and result in deadlock?

We could say that most battles and wars occur when people stop respecting differences in prejudices and start believing too much in their own story, their own idea. If you look at Bosnia-Herzegovina, Croatia, and Serbia, for example, each group feels strongly about its own ethnic pride and rights. Individuals have completely lost the realization that their own strong positions are intertwined with those of the other two groups. Their very passion derives and is sustained by the passion of the others. Therefore, no dialogue can occur, only escalation.

Another question that becomes interesting to us is how some people are able to view their idea only as prejudice, as one possible story, and not as "the truth." How is it some can compromise? This ability for acceptance of difference can be seen in recent historic developments in Western democracies. It is only of late that Western democracies have had some limited success in allowing people to express strongly opposing ideas, opinions, and prejudices and resolve their differences peacefully. One example can be seen in the United States, where there are very different views on abortion, yet somehow they are able to battle it out in dialogue rather than in the streets, with only an occasional eruption of violence. The democratic process still remains intact. There are many opposing views and prejudices in a democratic culture, but this is possible because of a general agreement to respect individual rights to disagree.

For therapists this ability may come with experience when one realizes that some prejudices and models are helpful in certain situations and not in others. Elsewhere (Cecchin et al., 1992), we have highlighted the potential danger involved when a therapist becomes too fanatical about any particular model because, when this occurs, in effect he or she places adherence to the model above the client. He or she runs the risk of being able to see only through the filter of the model. When, for whatever reason, therapy is not progressing as it is supposed to according to the model, the therapist is often unable to make a shift and temporarily let go of the model in order to act differently.

Another way for the therapist to develop this position of accepting different prejudices, or getting away from the search for truth, is to live in other cultures, or to visit other cultures and see that there are many different ways to survive. In democratic societies, for instance, strongly held prejudices may come out that are extremely different, even oppositional to one another. And yet the people who are in intense opposition are able to conduct dialogue with one another without an uncontrollable escalation taking place.

As systemic therapists our position is to accept doubt and somehow learn to live with it—doubt about theory, doubt about practice. However, our position regarding doubt is not to be seen as negative, but as something that is useful for therapists always to have a little doubt about what they are believing, what they are seeing, in order to prevent themselves from becoming fanatics and therefore dangerous to their clients.

If you are very insecure, you must hang on to the truth. If you are able to have doubts, then we think you are more secure. Somehow you are in a context in which you do not have to be a "true believer". Therapists who are able to maintain doubt usually have some stability in their life. They have a steady income, their life is not being threatened. Their future looks a little more positive.

If, for example, you are living in Iraq and you are threatened by a world superpower, then it is very hard to have doubt. Prior to the war between the United States, the allies, and Iraq, there was a great deal of animosity within Iraq towards Saddam Hussein. However, after the war began, the people in Iraq felt under a tremendous threat, and therefore were transformed into loyal followers, true believers. When individuals are under threat, or view themselves as being threatened, they tend to rally around what we might consider a radical leader who represents certainty. Germany under Hitler is another example.

For the sake of discussion, we will describe two of the many different prejudices held by therapists that a family in crisis might find when they come to therapy in search of certainty and security.

First, the family may meet a therapist who does not believe in taking charge of people's lives but, rather, encourages them to find their own solutions. An escalation can occur where the more the family insists the therapist take charge, the more he may insist they find their own solution. At times, this therapeutic orientation works. But often it leads to a useless, frustrating experience ending with accusations of deep pathology by the therapist towards the client, and counter accusations of incompetence by the client towards the therapist.

Second, they may meet a therapist who agrees with the family that they need someone with authority to take charge during this difficult moment in their lives. In this case things could also work out very well. Once the family have regained their confidence in their own resources they can leave therapy satisfied. However, more often than not the family can become convinced of their own helplessness and addicted to the therapist's leadership. Again, the therapist could accuse the family of being even more ill than he had realized. Or the family may increase their need for the therapist to the point where they accuse the therapist of not being accessible enough.

Let us fantasize, for a moment, how these two cases might have been different if a team or consultant had been assisting. In the first instance the therapist could be engaged in a dialogue with the team about his apparent excessive loyalty to the idea that people should take care of themselves. In such a conversation the discussion would highlight some of the potential consequences of sticking to this position. No direct suggestions would be made to the therapist; however, we might expect that he could do one of two things. First, the therapist could pose such questions to the family as "I know you would like me to take charge of your decisions at this moment. But let's talk about some of the consequences if I accepted your request." Second, the therapist might say something like "I must be honest with you. It is against my grain to take care of people because I deeply believe that no matter how desperate things appear, families always have resources to draw from, even if we don't see them at this moment."

In the second case, we could have a similar conversation within the team, and an imaginative alternative could be the therapist saying something like "When I see people in your condition it is a natural impulse for me to want to take charge. But my team warns me that this can lead to my becoming addicted to my own sense of authority in relation to you. I have to warn you that once I begin taking charge I sometimes go overboard and become like an overly intrusive parent. Therefore, I will agree to take authority temporarily, but I'm going to need you to help me out. I can't have the luxury of a team or consultant working with me all the time, and I want to ask for your help. If you see any sign of me becoming bossy, let me know before you get disgusted with me and drop out of therapy." Other strategies that can be used during a team discussion, or during self-reflection when a team or consultant is not available, which can be useful for breaking out of these kinds of impoverishing impasses will be described further as we go on.

Following the reasoning described above, when families come into therapy voicing very rigid prejudices we could easily assume that, frequently, this is a sign of great insecurity. The therapist can develop a sense of respect for this insecurity. The more fanatical the clients are about their prejudices, the more insecure we can usually assume they are. In such instances, we can become curious about the possibility of insecurity instead of being intimidated by their rigidity. This can help us avoid being seduced into a useless symmetrical escalation which often results in further intransigence. Why is it necessary for them to hang on to their stories so vitally, even if it means offending the culture, even if it means isolating themselves from the community? Our experience is that when families or clients hang on to a prejudice so tenaciously, usually their very identity is deeply wrapped up in their prejudice. They frequently feel they cannot exist without this prejudice.

It seems that, for many, belief in something is better than accepting the void of the unknown (Jackson, 1967c). This seems true, even with belief in obviously dangerous ideas, such as Jim Jones in

Guiana; or Pol Pot and the killing fields of Cambodia; or the bloodletting currently going on across Eastern Europe in the name of ethnic cleansing since the collapse of communist ideology and social control.

Going back to the family, we can recognize that people hold many different kinds of prejudices. Some of the most common ones we have experienced are:

• parents should control children

• mothers must always be loving

• children should be let free to grow up as they want

• fathers should be firm and in charge

• blood is thicker than water

• family secrets should not be shared with outsiders

• there should be no closed doors inside the home

• the authority and integrity of the grandparent is beyond question

• children are the property of parents

• children are the property of the state

• all we need is love

• disagreement equals disintegration of the family

• we all have to believe in the same god in the same way

The therapist represents a danger to these kinds of beliefs, especially when the therapist's prejudices are as strongly held as the client's. Some prejudices commonly held by therapists are:

• the family hierarchy must be correct

• the unconscious rules all

• open communication is the road to a happy marriage

• gender inequality is the source of all problems

• hierarchy inequality is the source of all problems

• most women who show signs of depression have been sexually abused (particularly in the United States)

- abstinence is the only proper goal of addiction treatment
- families are autonomous entities that should be allowed to develop their own idiosyncratic style
- the larger cultural system is responsible for making sure that parents raise their children correctly
- the state is responsible for the well-being of families
- current family problems are always connected to patterns in the family of origin
- the therapist's job is to re-parent defectively parented people
- the function of therapy is to help people recapture time lost
- families are dysfunctional and we are all co-dependent
- the inner-child has been damaged by the parents and healing
- therapy must be brief to be effective
- it takes years of intensive work to achieve substantial change
- only people with good insurance can benefit from therapy
- the state should provide total coverage for all mental health and relational complaints

Readers are encouraged to consider what their own prejudices may be, drawing from this partial list or by adding some of their own, and to reflect upon the logical implications of their prejudices.

Taking into consideration our bias that the therapist's prejudices influence his behaviour with clients, it is apparent that in the practice of therapy it becomes important how the initial dialogue with the family takes place. How the therapist first goes about attempting to understand the prejudices of the family without imposing his or her prejudice too rapidly is a delicate affair. Between these two sets of prejudices, those of the family members and those of the therapist, a tension occurs which is, for us, the essence of therapy. It is important to strive to maintain a working level of tension, rather than allowing it to shift into a rigid impasse.

We can imagine three ways these tensions can be handled. First, the differences in belief can rapidly move to the point of destructive impasse. Second, the therapist agrees completely with the ideology of the client—or the reverse, the client accepts completely the therapist's view—finding a syrupy, nice pleasantness that becomes flat and unproductive (the art of bringing this kind of pseudo-progress about could be one way of building a boring, but thriving practice). A third possibility that we like better is the artful maintenance of a healthy level of tension between different ideas, a tension that we believe can favour constructive reorganization and development of a larger requisite variety of alternatives for the client.

Perhaps an important difference between the prejudices of the client and the biases of the therapist is that the therapist can afford the luxury of doubt more easily than the family. In particular, if therapists are experienced and working in a safe environment that encourages openness and mutual confirmation, they can afford to be disrespectful to the truthfulness of their own beliefs. We can think of two contexts where the luxury of doubt is more difficult to achieve. One is when you work in a context with a rigid ideology where the maintenance of a clear, unequivocal image of the institution prevails over the open disclosure of doubt by the practitioners working there. In other words, the dogma of the institution prevails over and, to some extent, dictates the therapist's practice. The second instance involves beginning therapists, who cannot afford the luxury of doubt because they have not yet learned a model (a tautology of prejudices) or have not yet been able to distinguish between their model and strongly held personal prejudices. They are more insecure and therefore need the certainty of belief in one model.

We believe that the prejudices one constructs affect one's behaviour in clinical practice, as well as in one's personal life. This is inevitable. But for the sake of simplicity, when we refer to our prejudices in this book, we are referring to the prejudices that inform our clinical behaviour.

It may appear to some that we are going against the whole tradition of family therapy by pushing therapists of all schools to discuss their own prejudices at the risk of making them uncomfortable. After all, one of the reasons for the rapid growth of the family therapy movement was its rejection of traditional psychoanalytical premises, such as the mandate that a therapist should undergo sometimes painful, and always costly, personal analysis. We *are not* advocating a return to a time-consuming, expensive, personal analysis for the therapist. We are suggesting that it is very important to acknowledge and discuss how the therapist's actions are a product of his prejudices in the real-time moment of therapy. From our view this expedites, rather than prolongs therapy.

In the next chapter we delineate some of the beliefs and biases that guide our work.

Learning Resources
Centre

CHAPTER THREE

Clinical prejudices

There are practical consequences of prejudices in the context of therapy. Realizing the distinction between thought and action is an arbitrary one; we draw this dichotomy for the purpose of describing our practices of therapy. In reflexive fashion, prejudices reveal themselves through actions and the practices of therapy and vice versa.

The post ideological orientation we are introducing is based on the luxury of doubt. We believe this orientation is somewhat purist in the sense that we are only interested in the relationship and the context of how prejudices of the therapist interact and affect each other within the therapist's head and among his or her contemporaries; how the client's prejudices interact and affect each other, and how these two sets of prejudices interact with one another in a kind of cybernetics of prejudices. The relationship between these prejudices, not the content, becomes very important for us.

By now we hope the reader understands our belief that one cannot not have prejudices. Having described our theory, we now feel free to outline a non-exhaustive list of some of the beliefs that direct our clinical practice.

a.   Reinventing the one-way screen—
a mirror that reflects the prejudices of the therapist

The use of the one-way screen and teams acquires a different meaning. Originally born as a way to help the therapist observe the family from a different perspective for the purpose of helping them formulate better interventions, the mirror was then used extensively as an instrument for supervision. More recently the one-way screen has fallen into discredit in the eyes of some people of the non-instrumental movement (Anderson & Goolishian, 1988; Hoffman, 1986), who have come to view the screen as a secretive strategic technique that enhances the power of the therapist to force change. We can now reinvent the mirror as an instrument that can be used to help therapists become aware of their own prejudices. Being able to see in a real mirror his or her own biases, the therapist can begin to question them. Rather than pretending these biases do not exist, they can be put to use with the family.

Naturally this requires a therapist able to risk showing himself or herself openly to colleagues, and colleagues who are able to discuss differing prejudices without hint of criticism or gamesmanship. This kind of intellectual disrobing requires a deeply held conviction (bias) that *any* idea has an equal right and dignity in a conversation. How this is done requires time and practice, a sense of playfulness, irreverence, and reverence for the dignity and right of colleagues to hold differing views. A conversation is a system that can be productive only if any idea has equal dignity in relation to any other. Here content prevails over any sense of a hierarchical relationship. Competition recedes into a secondary position. Autism leads nowhere; the best way to learn about oneself is to mirror one's face to that of another willing to listen and talk. Of course, we confess that it is not easy to organize these kinds of conversations, because in most institutions content is used to re-establish and confirm hierarchical lines of power and control.

b. Just as one cannot not communicate,
one cannot not have a prejudice

All your life, particularly childhood and adolescence, is spent learning and acquiring ideas that help you to deal with friendly and unfriendly events. Without these constructions you could not survive. Reflecting back on our own orientation, we find it is partially rooted in Western democratic philosophy, an Eastern philosophical position of acceptance of things as they are, Batesonian systemic thinking, as well as constructionism. Combining these seemingly oppositional philosophies is our challenge.

It is difficult to have a conversation with people who hold that their bias is superior (or inferior) to your own. We believe that when people are unwilling to entertain alternative views they often either feel under threat, feel no vital interest in the relationship and no compelling reason to discuss differences, or simply feel so inferior or superior that differences are not ripe for discussion at that moment. A problem we frequently encounter is that people are not easily willing to reveal their prejudices and put them up for discussion. This is understandable. The conditions in which a person is able to reveal their prejudices freely are rare. We are all surrounded by other people whom we care about and have a vital interest in, and who, rather than viewing their own beliefs as prejudices, hold them as anchors to their identity—that is, as truths. None of us is immune.

Our experience is that people are often unwilling to share their most sacredly held prejudices because to do so may threaten even their most intimate relationships. But, this is an illusion—our prejudices reveal themselves, whether we want them to or not, sooner or later, in our words, actions—in how we live our lives. They seep through our pretences, coming out in our relationships with others—revealed more by what we do than what we say.

In relationships of vital interest to those involved (marital, parental, work, therapeutic, etc.), we feel it is dangerous not to be willing to put different strongly held opinions on the table for discussion. There is, however, a reflexive loop involved here. Even strong opinions, secretly held, are constructed through processes of interactions with others holding equally strong biases—prejudices do not arise in a void. Our therapeutic prejudice is that the function of therapy is to open up the flow of interaction between strong opinions. Strongly held biases can evolve into isolation or escalating fights for prominence, either of which, according to our bias, can contribute to the creation of suffering and pain in human systems. Diathesis, the bringing together of two theses (Rademeyer, personal communication 1992), seems an excellent word to describe the process we prefer. People cannot reconsider their prejudices when they feel they are under threat.

c. A person has worth because he exists

As therapists working in an open world we may find ourselves faced with seemingly hopeless situations in which the person involved may be hostile, uncooperative, or even repulsive. Or there may be politically loaded situations such as accusations of child molestation where the therapists may feel compelled to act in a specific way, homicide, threatened suicide, requests for medications, hospitalizations, electroconvulsant shock treatments, etc. From nurturing to cannibalism, human beings and organizations of human beings (including families) are capable of any behaviour imaginable. In other words, in certain situations the therapist may feel overwhelmed by the seeming hopelessness of the situation.

One idea that has helped us regain the ability to work in such situations is the bias that a person has worth merely because he exists. When you are able to view the person as having worth, regardless of the "hopeless" facts of the situation, you can regain interest in understanding the fellow humans in front of you, becoming curious about the persons—their relationships and contexts of living. As the therapist changes his or her own beliefs and biases about the client he or she becomes free to see the client differently—with less blame and less isolating condemnation. In one sense we agree with Jackson, who said, "How crazy a particular person appears to you depends on your own frame of reference and the limits of your own experience . . ." (1967e, p. 28).

The bias that a person has worth merely because he exists may be found in many traditions, from the early Greek Stoic philosopher Epictetus, to Christianity, to the systemic and constructivist literature. For us the best phrasing of this bias is the systemic, which posits that as long as a system exists each member of the system is of fundamental importance to its viability.

In discussing this prejudice we came to the conclusion that some readers will conclude that we are either fools or saints—and we are neither. We hold this prejudice to convey that we refuse to stop talking with people, even those who are in the seemingly worst, hopeless condition. If one takes this bias seriously, then the need or responsibility to control extreme behaviour is reduced.

d.   Control and its limitations

Apparent successes in controlling others, or being controlled by others, always seem to result in costly inefficiency, violence, and corruption. We believe that controlling mental patients, misbehaving adolescents, wilful children and ineffective parents, battering husbands and battered wives, oppressive employers and oppressed employees, and other "unruly" populations, not to mention alcohol and drug addicts (who we all *know* must be controlled), can only be done at extreme costs and, in the long run, never works. A father (although we *know* it is usually the mother) who insists he knows better than the child how the child must think and act, perhaps hoping that the child will grow up the "right way", often ends up spending tremendous amounts of money and time (in the form of psychiatric or legal fees) keeping the child subservient to his will. It can be done but at what cost? The same tyranny of logic can be seen in the Mafia's attempts to retain control over a territory, which ends up making the population apparently obedient but definitely less productive. In politics, there are numerous examples of the long-term inefficiency of control—from Stalinist Russia to Saddam Hussein's Iraq, the fact that crime rates fluctuate independently of the degree of control placed upon certain behaviours (most evident in the classical example of prohibition in the United States), and Bush's effort to control Saddam Hussein. The pathology of seeing another as needing to be controlled feeds the madness that one has to control. Efficiency, if it exists at all, seems to lie in the promotion of deviant individual elements of the population at the expense of all those involved. For example, prohibiting the sale and use of certain products (be it pornography, drugs, prostitution, etc.) often results in the creation of wealthy and powerful individuals who gain prestige at the expense of citizens who organize their existence around the consumption of such pacifiers.

What believers in the ability to control seem to forget is that nothing occurs a-historically. Every coercive relationship arises in a context. We are always looking for good guys and bad guys and in doing so end up creating circumstances in which the only "logical" solution is to control the situation.

Here we feel compelled to distinguish between attempts to control and the establishment of limits for behaviour that will be allowed to occur. Every human system must decide what will and will not be allowed to occur in a relationship. These are the limits that every social entity creates for itself. When these self-created limits are exceeded, consequences result or the rules guiding the system shift to incorporate the new behaviour. This is the brilliant insight of the early system thinkers (Jackson, Bateson, etc.). But the idea of limits should not be confused with the notion of simple control. Limits are parameters that emerge from the give and take of participants deciding together the limits. Difficulties arise when an individual presumes that he or she possesses the ability to impose limits on the system arbitrarily, that is, to dictate the parameters.

We believe that if children obey their parents, it is not because the parents make them do it. Rather, it is only due to parents having helped co-create a context of cooperation in which children are willing to agree to obey. The situation is similar between employees and their bosses, or between patients and their therapists.

e.   *No matter how much you try,*
     the illusion of influence
     and manipulation is unavoidable

How can a mother give up the illusion that if her child grows up well she is responsible for it? How can a therapist not feel proud when a client improves? How can a judge not feel responsible when a criminal repents (or returns to the judicial system after receiving a light reprimand). The illusion that we influence others is a fundamental belief of relational existence. We would not become professional therapists, stockbrokers, politicians, or anything else if we did not believe we had the ability to convince others to be loyal followers. While it seems true that humans do in fact influence one another, the sad fact is, however, that we cannot predict the outcome of our manipulations. God save the therapist (and his clients) who falls to the illusion that he has the ability to predict the effects of his actions.

How can we move away from the illusion that we have manipulated reality? Influencing one another is unavoidable. We cannot not influence one another. Many clients come to therapists because they have been unable to realize that their efforts to manipulate significant others do not always succeed: frustrated wives unable to influence husbands; frustrated parents unable to influence their children intentionally. A child-like belief that we have the ability to influence others in a predictable way feeds the ancient hubris that we have God-like powers.

How can therapists who are deluded into believing that they have the omnipotent ability to influence clients help clients experiencing the same kind of delusions? Sometimes therapy ends successfully when clients attain the ability to see themselves as actors (able to influence their situation). This belief is very good for some clients. Should such a belief be challenged or bolstered? When one is able to deconstruct one's own mythologies of change, therapy, and influence, then one is free to engage the client in a lively, ironic, and irreverent improvisational interaction. This is the essence of a post-ideological orientation in therapy.

Our movement into a post-ideological orientation came primarily from the irreverence of our clients. Clients, by and large, are far less inhibited than therapists. Our attempts to free ourselves from the temptation of belief in our ability to evoke change in a predictive way is helped tremendously by these clients. To a large extent, clients want to see someone who will be helpful to them, and the ideological orientation of the therapist is of little concern to them.

f.   Topology is a fascinating myth about the past which has nothing to do with the future

When we began to discuss the notion of classification and topology, at first glance it seemed a simple topic about which we would have very little to say. But as we tried to write down a simple description of our thoughts about classification we became involved in a conversation involving a number of levels of abstraction, from the most basic to the most abstract. The implications of classification led us from simplicity to a temporary autism, unable to put into words our multiple views of topology.

Classification—the process of drawing distinctions, of organizing experience and observations, so as to comprehend and act—seems to have been a major preoccupation for humans since the beginning of recorded time. From Aristotle on, it has been the dominant activity of science, religion, and philosophy as humankind has attempted to make sense of and describe the world around us.

We respect those colleagues who follow a traditional, rigorous orientation towards nosology and classification. For example, biochemical research is important; genetic research is equally intriguing. Researchers utilize classification systems to investigate microscopically the nature of nature, which obviously includes human interaction.

A problem arises, however, when attempts are made to apply abstract "findings" (or is it constructions?) of research in clinical work with clients. People will probably always search for understanding by Aristotelian partialization of complex phenomena. For us, however, the utility of this scientific knowledge in clinical practice is highly questionable. When you step into the therapy room to speak with a particular family, such statistical research on probabilities is not useful. Research and classification belong to one logical level of description. Translating these findings into actions, however, necessarily involves shifting to a another logical level. We agree with Bateson (1972) that to attempt to apply research findings as a basis for therapeutic conduct is an error in logic fraught with potentially tragic consequences.

We consider ourselves frivolous users of traditional classification systems. By frivolous we mean that we view and utilize the concretized findings of "hard" science as the popular culture might do. For example, we use in non-rigorous fashion such words as depressed, manic, co-dependent, addicted, hyperactive, and so forth, because a post-ideological language is not yet well formulated. Perhaps it is to our advantage that there is not a well-defined post-ideological language, because if one existed we might run the risk of over-reifications and concretization again. Therefore, we prefer to stick with our frivolous usage, constantly reminding each other that our usage of these terms is based only on our temporary biases about that person at that moment in time, not as definitive labels about the nature of someone or some interactive process, but rather only as temporary attempts to make sense of what is going on at the moment.

g.   We do not believe in
successful outcomes in therapy

We are impressed, within the genre of therapy called family therapy and brief therapy, by how many clinicians, theorists, and researchers attempt to demonstrate the validity of a given orientation through outcome studies. The whole logic of talking about successful outcomes in therapy seems, to us, suspect, particularly in light of the fact that throughout the behavioural sciences these claims of successful outcomes by family and brief therapy are not accepted as credible by insurance companies, psychiatry, and other medical professions. At best, family therapy and brief therapy continue to be viewed as techniques and methods—not that other orientations can claim any better success in their outcome studies.

It appears that our field is possessed by a necessity to prove its worth by means of displaying its successes. The more established mental health disciplines do not seem to find it necessary to prove their merit. Psychoanalysis, biochemical and pharmacological psychiatry, and so forth seem to be flourishing with little or no conclusive evidence of their effectiveness (Jackson, 1960, 1967e; Laing, 1971). In many ways the mental health disciplines, including a large part of family therapy, have done little to demonstrate that their diagnostic and treatment methodologies are little more than searches for pathologies aimed at proving that the ill are different from us professionals who are, of course, normal. Szasz (1970) succinctly summarizes these sentiments:

> . . . there is no behavior or person that a modern psychiatrist cannot plausibly diagnose as mentally ill. . . . Certainly, there is no childhood behavior that a psychiatrist could not place in one of these categories. To classify as pathological academic performance that is "under-achievement," "over-achievement," or "erratic performance" would be humorous were it not tragic. When we are told that if a psychiatric patient is early for his appointment he is anxious, if late he is hostile, and on time, compulsive—we laugh, because it is supposed to be a joke. But here we are told the same thing in all seriousness. . . . It is necessary to recall here the economic aspects of the witch hunts. [p. 35]

It seems to us that therapy, in all of its many forms, will continue to thrive, regardless of the ability to prove its effectiveness through official outcome studies. In those instances when a client and a therapist feel they have achieved a desired outcome, quantifying precisely *what* and *how* it happened can never be known. It is a mystery the explanation of which only obscures the beauty of the experience. Furthermore, the warnings of Bateson, Maturana, and others about the dangers of intentional interventions in terms of their long-term impact on ecologies continue to haunt us. If convincing research data were available we would have the luxury of non-accountability. But, fortunately, no such irrefutable data exist, regardless of the growing number of pseudo-scientific therapists who make grandiose claims of having discovered such proofs.

This means that the only weapon we have is to be accountable for our actions. If we did not believe ourselves to be helpful to clients, each of us would find other ways to make a living. It does not excuse us from striving to understand how to conduct ourselves in resourceful ways with clients—by generating working hypotheses, and experimenting with novel ways to understand situations and enabling people to change in ecologically coherent ways.

When therapists or students become obsessed with figuring out exactly what works or doesn't work (obviously so that it can be either replicated or outlawed), they lose sight of what we believe is more relevant: that is, where context and pattern are involved, there is no "right" question or "more correct" answer. What do you have? You have a system that is coherent, self-organizing, and absolutely successful in maintaining its own stability.

There are, then, two general ways to approach therapy. One way seems to be fascinated with codifying specific methods for changing clients. The other is to be more interested in understanding how a family has succeeded in organizing itself in such a way as to be what it is, and to give consideration to the possible ramifications of our assertions therapeutically before rushing in and doing something.

h.   Circular questions:
bringing forth the prejudices
of the therapist and the family

Circular questions remain one of the most useful, non-confrontational, ways for bringing forth and relating the biases of the therapist and the family. The prejudices of the therapist and family come out naturally. Asking questions in a circular manner juxtaposes these sets of biases. We try to create a context in which the family do not have to fight to defend their prejudices, but are free to examine the consequences of them. The therapist is not attacking them but tries to create a context in which the prejudices of the family and the therapist are juxtaposed and examined in relationship to one another. In this way, you can permit yourself the luxury of doubt, which does not necessarily interfere with holding the strong opinions that are the salt of life. How one can have strong beliefs without trying to force them on others becomes the therapist's challenge.

Searching for pathology is useless—rather, by means of circular questioning, seek out the implications of prejudices. Be curious about patterns not "facts". For further elaboration of the concept of circular questioning see Cecchin (1987) and Palazzoli, Boscolo, Cecchin, and Prata (1980).

i.   Be useful, not helpful

In general, we believe that to be useful is not the same as to be helpful. This means that, at times, not being helpful is very useful. Naive helping assumes and implies that a handicap exists on the part of the receiver (client). Therapists who view the client in this way often convey an attitude that the client is lacking some skill or resource that the therapist possesses and can lend to the client. Taking such a position implies that the therapist is healthy and the client is not. This is why we prefer the term useful rather than helpful. People come to us for help, and we usually try to respond by being useful.

j.   Utilize temporary certainty

We do not advocate that people should become irresolute with their beliefs. On the contrary, we believe that people are naturally passionate about their beliefs. One bias we hold is that it is often useful to place a time limit around passionate beliefs, or recognize that if the context changes the belief may have to change too. An example would be the story about the family patriarch who proclaimed in a session, "No one spends money in this family without my approval as long as I live." Two weeks later his son drove to the scheduled therapy session in his new Porsche, directly from his father's funeral service.

There are many instances in therapy where the idea of temporary certainty is useful. For instance, a client in her late twenties came to therapy because she felt she was a failure. In defining the goals of therapy she requested that the therapist help her to improve her self-esteem, to have more confidence in herself in social situations, and to overcome an intense fear of making wrong decisions and destroying her own future. She was asked who in her life would have the most difficulty adapting once she began to achieve some of her goals, to which she immediately replied "my father". She then explained that her father felt responsible for her, enjoyed helping her out when she needed help financially, etc. She went on to say that her worst fear was the thought of losing her mother and father (who were growing old and were in questionable health).

The therapist was pleased at this revelation. His belief in many of the fundamental family therapy tenets were reinforced, and he was certain that helping the client attain more independence from the parents would be a relatively simple matter. He talked with the client about the usefulness of going slow in her efforts to attain autonomy, in order to avoid upsetting her parents, thinking that doing this would surely have the strategic and paradoxical effect of freeing her up to change.

One year later, he decided to consult with his treatment team to figure out why therapy with the young woman was going no-where. It took a lot of work on the part of his colleagues to break through the stubborn certainty of the therapist that a more inde-pendent behaviour on the part of the client was necessary for her personal growth. Hours of persuasion were necessary to bring the therapist to adopt a position, at least temporarily, that the girl needed to continue her role as a daughter, which she knew how to do very well, and which was continually reinforced by the parents (and had inadvertently been reinforced by the therapist's symbolic symmetrical competition with the parents by giving messages that becoming independent was better than remaining a daughter). Pos-sibly, the insistence on the part of the therapist that she become more independent was being interpreted by the client as an invita-tion to betray her parents, which as a good daughter she could never do.

In the next session the therapist explained this new understand-ing to the young woman, even asking the client to help him out by noticing if she caught him relapsing back into his old, sticky con-ventionality that she should be more independent. After this conversation, therapy began to acquire a new life.

Basically, every prejudice is temporary because it is constantly interacting with the prejudices of others. However, when two prejudices become interlocked in a mutually reinforcing way, noth-ing can change. The two extremes of sticking tenaciously with beliefs are to become either a hero or a fanatic.

k.   Only with accountability is a civilized society possible

It is very difficult in the therapeutic culture not to be seduced into thinking about how things should be, rather than focusing more on how things are. There seems to be a human tendency to think in terms of how things should be. The media bombard us with reasons for why we should change—commercials telling us how to exercise, what to eat to have a healthy diet, etc. Politicians explain why we should vote against or for this or that. News commentators tell us what the Russians should do, what the Serbs should do, what the U.S. President should do. You would think that with all this good advice our problems would be evaporating before our eyes. Opinions dominate our culture about how things would be better if only the other person would do as some self-elected expert thinks they should.

The same kind of atmosphere dominates the therapeutic culture, where everyone seems to be waiting for everyone else to act the way they should, according to some preconceived ideal, rather than thinking about the ramifications of how things are right now. The tendency to make plans for the future seems a natural one. But excessive concern for what should be makes it impossible to pay attention to how things are. For us, the royal road to becoming alive as a human being is to reflect on our own prejudices in relation to the prejudices of others *before* attempting to look into the future.

In attempting to keep focus on how systems such as families have achieved their current style of organization, the problem is to avoid shifting into being moralistic reformers who insist that "improvement" equals adoption of one of their particular biases. And here we come to the problem of accountability. The person who takes the position of a reformer *appears* to be the most responsible one. However, this is an illusion. There are great difficulties with the logic of reform. In an article entitled "The Dramatization of Evil", Tannenbaum (1938) expressed a concern similar in many respects to our own:

> In the conflict between the young delinquent and the community there develop two opposing definitions of the situation. By the delinquent . . . breaking windows, annoying people, playing

truant all are items of play, adventure, excitement. To the community, however, these activities may and often do take on the form of nuisance, evil, delinquency, with the demand for control [and] punishment. This conflict over the situation arises out of a divergence of values. As the problem develops, the situation gradually becomes redefined. The attitude of the community hardens definitely into a demand for suppression. There is a gradual shift from the definition of specific acts as evil to a definition of the individual as evil, so that all his acts come to be looked upon with suspicion. In the process of identification ... all his conduct becomes subject to scrutiny and question. From the community's point of view the individual, who used to do bad and mischievous things, has now become a bad and unredeemable human being. From the individual's point of view there has taken place a similar change. He has gone slowly from a sense of grievance and injustice to a recognition that the definition of him as a human being is different from that of other boys in his community. It becomes, in part a process of rationalization, in part a simple response to a specialized type of stimulus. The young delinquent becomes bad because he is defined as bad and because he is not believed if he is good. There is a persistent demand for consistency in character. The community cannot deal with people it cannot define. Reputation is this sort of public definition. Once established then unconsciously *all* agencies combine to maintain this definition even when they apparently and consciously attempt to deny their implicit judgement. The first dramatization of the "evil" which separates the child out of his group for specialized treatment plays a greater role in making the criminal than perhaps any other experience. It cannot be too often emphasized that for the child the whole situation has become different. He now lives in a different world. He has been tagged. A new and hitherto nonexistent environment has been precipitated out for him.

The process of making the criminal, therefore, is a process of tagging, defining, identifying, segregating, describing, emphasizing, making conscious and self-conscious; it becomes a way of stimulating, emphasizing, and evoking the very traits that are complained of. If the theory of relation of response to stimulus has any meaning, the entire process of dealing with the young delinquent is mischievous in so far as it identifies him to himself and to the environment as a delinquent person. The person becomes the thing he is described as being. Nor does it matter whether the valuation is made by those who would punish or by those who would reform. In either case, the emphasis is upon the conduct that is disapproved of. The parents or the policemen, . . . in so far as they rest upon the thing complained of, rest upon a false ground. Their very enthusiasm defeats their aim. The harder they work to reform the evil, the greater the evil grows under their hands. The persistent suggestion, with whatever good intentions, works mischief because it leads to bringing out the bad behavior it would suppress. The way out is through a refusal to dramatize the evil. The less said about it the better. The more said about something else, still better. In dealing with the delinquent, therefore, the important thing to remember is that we are dealing with a human being who is responding normally to the demands, stimuli, approval, expectancy, of the group with whom he is associated. [pp. 19–20]

Before you can do any kind of reform you need to become aware of and responsible for your own biases that act to keep the system the way it is now. If you are not first willing to become aware of your own prejudices and how they come into play in relation to your clients, you will inadvertently set into motion an escalating process in which the very thing you hope to reform grows worse the more you try to change it. We want to emphasize that we are talking about a strongly held ethical position here, and not merely describing some simple strategic tactic.

An example that comes to mind involves a story told to us by a colleague about an inner-city church community which was located in an area that was at one time predominantly white. Over time the neighbourhood became predominantly populated by poor blacks, while the church congregation remained white. An inspired new minister, who was hired by the congregation, began to explain in his sermons that to be a Christian means to practise Christian love towards all people. One result was that a small group of church members began an outreach evangelical program with the aim of bringing food, clothing, and comfort to black families in need. To their surprise their well-intentioned charity was met with hostility and suspicion. Their rejection was brought up for discussion with the minister and the larger congregation. One of the church members came up with what we would call an irreverent proposal for solving the impasse: that the members of the evangelical group return to the black community and tell them that they had a problem. The problem was that they had a deep ingrained bias against blacks which they needed to acknowledge, but that their desire to carry out charitable acts was strong and related to their love for God which overrode their prejudice. To their great surprise they were met by a positive response. Some of the black people were able to acknowledge that they themselves did not like whites anyway, especially uninvited ones who intruded into their lives as missionaries. Once the two groups acknowledged their own deeply held biases, a more open relationship began to evolve between them based upon mutual respect and dignity. A few of the members even described what they felt was the emergence of a Christian love for their neighbours. In this real-life example, of course not all of the congregation were able to appreciate the value of this experience. Some remained loyal to an abstract Christian view that they should love everyone without question, and rather than face up to their own biases they decided to leave the congregation.

CHAPTER FOUR

Managing discourse about prejudices: the heart of therapy

As we described earlier, the process of the therapist coming to terms with his own prejudices is essential before launching into intervening into the lives of clients. One difficulty, however, is that often the therapist is not aware of the deeply ingrained prejudices he or she holds which inform the therapy he or she does.

In the cases we are about to describe we are not interested in providing elaborate examples of how each of the authors structures therapy or in providing stories about the techniques we use. The reader can find mountains of books (some written by us) describing what to do and what not to do in therapy. Rather, we will discuss our beginning attempts to move into a post-ideological process of questioning our own prejudices, and how our prejudices interact and affect each other within our own heads, how our own prejudices affect and are affected by and among our team members. We will then move to a discussion of the interaction between the therapist's and client's prejudices. While we will be addressing techniques per se, one suspicion we have, however, is that the very process of questioning our own prejudices and those of the client can be very therapeutic in and of itself. When the process of questioning our own prejudices is entered into, we often find ourselves not moving into the more traditional phases of therapeutic interventions that are the hallmarks of all models of therapy.

Several overviews of case examples—sketches of clinical situations—are presented below. These are not in-depth studies of cases; rather, sufficient information is provided about a case to be a backdrop for discussion of the interaction between therapist/team/client prejudices.

The case of the depressed brother

A therapist presented a case to our consulting team in which she was puzzled about what to do. She described a situation in which a female psychotherapist in her early twenties, who practised in a church or religious setting, requested a consultation. She described herself as a Christian counsellor. Her request was that she needed to help her 26-year-old brother leave home and get on with his life as she felt she had been able to do. According to her, her brother was frozen in time, depressed, and needed to take the next step in the life cycle—to move out and become more independent. The therapist accepted the story of the young woman, adding her own hypothesis that this was a highly enmeshed family. Having this belief, she agreed with the woman that her brother, at the age of 26, obviously needed to leave home and to get on with his life without the assistance of his parents. The daughter returned home and told her parents and brother that she had found a therapist who, she thought, could help them resolve her brother's depression.

The entire family was invited to the next session, during which the story came out that several months earlier the son had attempted to kill himself by slashing his wrists in the basement of the family home. The mother had found him wrapped in a white sheet and lying on the floor. She said that his appearance reminded her of Jesus after He was taken down from the cross. The story concerned the therapist so much she abandoned her belief that the son should move out immediately. Instead, she thought the young man should go into a psychiatric hospital in another state to be treated for his problems.

When this proposal was made, the mother became furious with the therapist and began to insult her, stating, "You must be incompetent, you don't know what you are doing, don't you realize that I love my son, that I need to take care of him." The therapist was stunned by the mother's reaction. She had assumed that since the father was a physician and the mother a retired nurse, they would agree with her assessment and follow her clinical prescription. Instead they rejected both. At this point the problem for the therapist was how to get the young man out of the family so that he could receive treatment for his depression and separation problem. The therapist was following the ideology that people need to be told how to solve problems, and she considered it her job to lead them towards a mentally healthier life.

During the consultation with the team, the story came out that the mother and son were deeply attached emotionally—in some ways it was as though they were married. It also came out that the daughter had left the family when she herself had begun therapy. After the daughter had left the home, the father, who appeared to have been emotionally married to the daughter, became very ill with multiple sclerosis and had to stop practising medicine. It took very little time for the consultation to help the therapist become aware of her prejudices in the case. It became very clear that the therapist was admiring the daughter's ability to grow up in what appeared to be a very enmeshed family, and accepted the daughter's premise that her brother needed help in leaving the family.

Initially the therapist viewed the family situation in a very straightforward manner—the family needed a traditional structural intervention—and she had focused on helping the son leave home. But when the therapist suggested this, the family began to attack her and she felt insulted. What emerged in the consultation group discussion might be considered the dark side of this family. The therapist even began to have some doubts about continuing to work with the family and said that she might refer them to a "Christian" counsellor, since they described themselves as a highly religious family.

It took little time for the consultation group to help the therapist see that her prejudices were affecting therapy in a very powerful way, that her beliefs and those of the family's had reached a point of extreme tension. The key was to find a way to continue the dialogue without a damaging escalation of prejudices. The therapist became aware of her anger at the parents for not allowing the children to grow up. She was also frustrated that the family did not accept what she considered to be a more healthy way of organizing their lives. She was able to acknowledge that she felt hurt when the family did not accept her prescription.

As we said earlier, often when clients do not accept a therapist's framing they are labelled by the therapist as being resistant and even more disturbed and pathological. It is a very natural process for the consultant or team to be able to see the stuck points of the therapist, and in this non-threatening context for the therapist to be able to be more aware of her own prejudices and feelings about the case. It was suggested that the therapist call the family and apologize for attempting to rush them into change and to apologize for trying to persuade them to do something they were not ready to do. Instead of seeing the son as helpless and incompetent, the team began to admire his abilities to help this family stay the same; how on some level he had dedicated himself loyally to maintaining the balance between his parents once his sister had left. The team also helped the therapist see how upset the father was about having lost his daughter, and how the mother was feeling threatened by the prospect of losing her son, to whom she appeared to be the closest.

Asking the son to leave at this moment was too far out of tune with the family music. The therapist began to trust herself and to feel that therapy was going well—the family had demonstrated great trust in her by revealing their tragic drama, as opposed to what initially was a rather superficial dilemma of simply leaving home.

Through the team consultation process, the therapist was able to become aware of her own prejudices and to begin to examine how they were interacting with the family story. Once this relationship of prejudices was brought into discussion, the therapy could proceed in a very lively, engaging manner.

The mistreated husband and the conventional wife

A middle-aged couple and their 20-year-old son came to therapy, sent by another couple who were also in therapy. The situation is a classical one in which two therapists, one male and one female, worked with the family while a team observed from behind a mirror. The team consisted of a teacher/lead expert and a group of student-practitioners. The therapists in the room were also student-practitioners.

The story arose in which the son gave up studying and being active socially, staying home all the time and complaining to his mother about his unhappiness and isolation. The father, a successful business executive, had been silently angry for months at both his wife and son, spending a lot of time fuming in silence when around them. The son, in answer to a question posed by one of the therapists, described his parents as the most unlikely couple in the world. From the son's view, his father expected his wife to be lively, intelligent, and vivacious—a person with whom he could enjoy conversations about art, politics, and other cultural topics. That was how she had appeared to him before they married. But, according to the son, his mother had ended up being a conventional housewife, busy with cleaning, cooking, enjoying superficial chats with other neighbourhood housewives, and other mundane activities. The son went on to say that he felt his mother was also very disappointed in the father. She had expected her husband to be a nurturing, attentive man. But she found herself living with a cold man who spent most of his time busy with his books and computer. The son said his parents stayed together only because he was alive.

When asked to comment on what their son had said both parents enthusiastically agreed with him. The male therapist puzzled with the family about how they could live together this way. He asked about their daily routine and habits of living together. What emerged was that the husband came home twice a day to have lunch and dinner with his wife. They had very few friends. The husband spent most evenings at home not talking with his wife or son. During the day the wife would spend time talking with other housewives in the neighbourhood.

The two therapists left the room and joined the therapy team behind the mirror to discuss the family's situation. The lights were turned up in the team room so that the family could observe and listen to the team discussion (Ray, Keeney, Parker, & Pascal, 1992). Following our routine procedure, the first to speak were the two therapists, who were asked by the team leader to describe their feelings, ideas, and reactions to the family. The therapists agreed with each other that the marriage was not going well. The female therapist felt that the problem was that the husband was being ignored and mistreated by the wife, in deference to the son, and that something should be done about this. The male therapist took an opposite view. He thought the wife was being neglected by the husband and, being a lively woman, had increased her involvement with her son because her husband refused to nurture her. After the therapists had described their opinions, the other team members were invited to express theirs. One member of the team voiced the view that the son was right in thinking that he was keeping his parents together. Another team member took the position that he felt sorry for the family, who were so isolated from the community and alienated from each other. He thought therapy should focus on helping the family improve their communication skills.

Here we could see a wide range of diagnostic biases and fantasies among the team members about the family. The male therapist took a feminist bias that the wife was justified in feeling dominated by her chauvinist husband. The female therapist took a patriarchal bias that the wife should be more understanding of and available to her husband. One of the team members voiced an independence bias in which the problem was that the son needed to differentiate from his parents. Yet another took the view that the problem was poor communication and that therapy should focus on helping the family learn to share their feelings more openly. During this conversation the team leader was becoming restless since his own biases were being triggered as much by the team conversation as by the family situation. He erupted, voicing his own prejudice: "You members of the team, in everything you are saying, there is a constant and explicit demand that the family *should* be different from how they are. This is exactly what the family is stuck with— accusations towards each other that they *should* be different." But even the authoritative position voiced by the team leader was not sufficient to quell the opinions of the team members—one member of the team explicitly asked, "What is therapy supposed to be about? Aren't we supposed to help people by listening to their requests for help and then helping them solve these problems?" The leader insisted that the team find a way to describe the family without imposing conceptions of how they should be. He insisted that they should find ways to describe these people positively, as having dedicated their life to waiting for the other person to change. The state of waiting gave real meaning to their lives. In a way they showed tremendous respect and esteem for each other. It is quite a romantic story about people who were prepared to wait twenty or twenty-five years for their wife or husband to change. If they had had no esteem and admiration for the other, they would not have stayed together for so long. A less romantic couple would have given up and divorced long ago. What son would devote his life to waiting for his parents to have the kind of relationship he thinks they should have?

Astonished by what the team leader said, another member of the team exclaimed, "Do you really believe what you are saying? Or is this one of those positive connotation tricks I've heard you use? No one believes in that anymore do they?"

The teacher insisted that he strongly believed in the viewpoint that systems have their own logical explanations for being the way they are at any given moment in time. And if you look for it, you can find (or create) a logical explanation (in our experience, systemically logical explanations invariably end up giving value and dignity to the behaviour of those involved—as well as introducing a novel way of describing their situation). The teacher felt his position as team leader gave him the right to impose his prejudice on the rest of the team. Yet still another team member was equally adamant, asking, "Don't you think we give value and dignity to people by accepting their perception that their relationship is dysfunctional and it is our job to help them fix it?"

This conversation continued without resolution for about twenty-five minutes, at which time one of the therapists indicated that the time was up and they needed to rejoin the family, which they did. The family, especially the parents, appeared very amused and interested in what they had heard and soon declared that they had heard enough and were ready to leave. Upon asking for another appointment, the wife said, smiling, "I never thought we could be described as a romantic couple." The son, in contrast, said he was not sure he was going to come next time.

The interaction of the prejudices of various members of the team seemed to have some resonance with the multiple feelings of the family members. The family seemed able to tolerate the different views articulated by various members of the team. Perhaps the absence of any definitive "reform" or "reframing" message opened the possibility for the family to conceive of themselves differently. As can be seen in this example, our use of team discussion usually follows a particular structure: first, the therapist is asked to describe his or her reactions and impressions of the client. Then the other team members are invited to describe their views, opinions, and perceptions of the prejudices of the therapist, with the therapist listening but not participating in the talk. During this interaction the team leader monitors the conversation, attempting to intercede when negative descriptions begin to prevail. The team leader also decides when it is time to wrap up the discussion and to invite the therapist to comment on what has been said. The particular question posed to the therapist at this moment is, "Can you use what your colleagues have said?" After having the last word, the therapist rejoins the client to wrap up the session.

In instances where the team and therapist are not in formal training but are working together as equal participants, we encourage them to elect one member to take the job of monitor and gatekeeper.

In those many instances when a therapist is working without a team, we recommend that the therapist should take a break as is normally done and then hold an externalizing dialogue within himself or herself about multiple prejudices and views that might be involved in the case. At other times, although this takes more time, a therapist working alone can review the videotape or audio-recording of the session, think about the possible biases implicit in his or her work, and reflect them back to the family at the next session. In yet another variation, a student-practitioner who does not yet have the ability to interact with a team in vivo during therapy can videotape his subsequent consultation with a therapeutic team and play the tape of the team discussion back for the client at the next session. We have experimented with all of these variations quite successfully.

All leaders in the field are bound to have very strongly held prejudices which inform their view. Some of the predominant organizing biases popular in the field today include:

- the attempted solution is the problem
- the male-dominated society is the root problem
- we must tease out the attempted solutions and elaborate on them
- if we just talk to the client in imperceptible ways something will happen
- when in doubt ask what would happen if a miracle happened
- differentiate—take an "I" position
- the hierarchy is confused, etc.

An abused wife and the sympathetic therapist

An experienced family therapist came to a meeting of a consultation team and described the following situation. A family she had been working with for the past three months was becoming extremely frustrating and emotionally draining for her. The case involved a mother recently married for the second time. She had three children, two boys, ages 14 and 8 years, and a daughter age 4. The client had been referred for therapy by an attorney after she had initiated court proceedings to limit the custody privileges of the children's father. The primary presenting concern involved the 14-year-old son, who was described as depressed and progressively refusing to talk with the therapist in sessions. The therapist had tried having individual sessions with him, but he continued to talk less and less. She wanted the consultation team to help her develop a way to handle this silent and depressed client more effectively.

The therapist went on to relate that the mother had revealed that, while she had no hard evidence, she was convinced that during the first marriage the father had physically and mentally abused the children. She also described having been beaten by her first husband on a number of occasions. During therapy it came out that the mother, after twelve years of marriage, had had an affair with the man who would eventually become her second husband, subsequently leaving the two oldest children in the care of the first husband and moving across the country with her new lover and

4-year-old daughter. A year later the father gave permission for the two boys to live with their mother and the new step-father.

In order to be closer to the children, the biological father had recently moved to the same city as the mother and assumed his court-approved visitation rights with the children. The mother became convinced that the children might be abused again during visits with the father, as she thought they had been in the past. Her new husband agreed with her, and they refused to allow the children to visit their father. A battle erupted between the oldest son and the mother, with the son demanding to be allowed to see his father. The mother reluctantly allowed the son to resume weekend visits, but at the same time she increased her efforts to strip her former husband of all visitation privileges.

The therapist described herself as being very sympathetic to the mother with regard to the fear she had of her former husband, agreeing that the children may have been abused and also agreeing to testify as an expert witness for the mother against the father. This agreement between the therapist and mother was kept from the children to prevent them from becoming more upset. While describing the case to the consulting team, the therapist also mentioned, in passing, that she was a close personal friend of the mother's attorney.

After the therapist had described the case, the consulting team began to play with different ideas and hypotheses about the therapist's feeling of frustration and being stuck. Team members were sharing many questions about the situation, including whether the legal aspects and the suspicion of abuse were creating a blind curtain, making it difficult for the therapist to develop fresh ideas about the case. During the consultation some of the prejudices of the team members that were discussed were:

- What makes the therapist believe so strongly in the mother's story?
- Is the mother projecting her fears about the father onto the children?
- The oldest son seems more loyal to the father than the mother.
- Some members of the team brought up the idea that the attorney is a good referral source, and that the therapist seems to have some kind of obligation to the attorney.

- Other team members felt that the therapist was genuinely convinced by the mother that the abuse had taken place.

- The children have probably been abused and should be protected.

- What a lousy mother to abandon two of her children just to run off with her first husband's friend.

- The mother and step-father were using therapy to build a case against the husband in the courts.

- The boy's silence sends a loud message to his mother and her paid expert that he was not going to help against his dad.

- The therapist is unknowingly being exploited by the mother for legal purposes.

After this consultation with the team, the therapist decided to call the entire family into a session (mother, step-father, and the three children). The therapist announced that while she had tried very hard to remain neutral in the situation, she was not able to do so. She stated that she agreed with the mother that the children had probably been abused by the father. Then she turned and said to the 14-year-old son, "I realize that you love your father and are very loyal to him. I want you to be very clear that I am on your mother's side in this situation and not your father's. Therefore, coming to family therapy is a painful and impossible situation for you because, with a therapist who feels as strongly as I do, it may not be helpful for you to come to this therapy. So I am suggesting to your parents that you should be given the freedom not to come to these sessions, and, if you desire, they should find an individual therapist for you to see in complete confidentiality and separate from them."

For us, the important point of this story was that the therapist recognized and took responsibility for her strongly held bias for the mother. She did not pretend to be neutral, or able to support the boy's desire to support his father. She also realized that by forcing the child to come to therapy she would have been placing him in the untenable position of having to betray his father.

The conclusion of the case came in the courts when the presiding judge made the legal decision to allow the 14-year-old son to live with his father, which he did.

I'm a bum just like my father and grandfather

A therapist trainee was seeing a family during live supervision. The family came to therapy because the 16-year-old adolescent son was described as being poly-addicted. He had been thrown out of three treatment programmes because the treatment staff feared his violence—it was said that he had killed a dog with a bat and blown up a truck. He was living with a maternal aunt and uncle. His mother was described as being "loose" sexually and a "drunk", and she was living with a boyfriend who was also a drunk. The mother had divorced the father when the son was an infant, and the father had been out of the picture for years.

The therapist was a self-described recovering alcoholic enrolled in a two-year marriage and family therapy programme. Up until this point, therapy had centred on helping the adolescent remain abstinent and stay out of trouble in school and had danced around exploring the mythology of the potential violence of the son. In the session a big family secret was revealed: the maternal grandfather had been a severe alcoholic who was very violent. On several occasions he had nearly killed the grandmother by stabbing her and shooting her with a shotgun.

The aunt, grandmother, and mother had never told the children about the grandfather but regularly said to the 16-year-old boy that he was "just like your grandpa (i.e. violent and addicted). In turn, the grandmother was revered by family members for her "saintly" behaviour. Everyone was very protective towards her. It also came out that the 16-year-old's mother, who was now seen as the black sheep of the family, used to stand up for her siblings and protect them from the grandfather when he was being violent.

The boy was furious with his mother for not being more available to him. He also said that he tended to get nervous and would subsequently drink whenever the aunt, mother, or grandmother began to worry out loud about fearing he would relapse. In exploring the alleged violence of the son, it turned out that the stories of violence had been exaggerated—he had not blown up a truck, but rather had blown up the engine while driving too fast. He had killed a dog with a bat, but in self-defence after having been attacked by the dog.

The team decided to take a break and converse in private about the family's situation. There was a long period of silence because the entire team felt overwhelmed by the family story. Slowly they began to talk about the different feelings and prejudices related to the case. One member was very annoyed by what he thought was irresponsible behaviour on the part of the boy's mother. He expressed his feeling that therapy was futile with such enmeshed, self-destructive people. Another member said that the family probably only came to therapy to help the boy avoid going to jail. One opinion was that this boy was dangerous and possibly a hopeless psychopath who came to therapy to avoid justice. Another was that with a mother who was so irresponsible and promiscuous, little wonder this son was a drug addict. And the idea was put forward that in a family like this there was very little space for a male to gain a position of dignity and worth in the shadow of the grandfather's history of violence and drunkenness, and the father's history of abandonment. Another team member conjectured that the grandmother was exploiting the grandson in order to punish her daughter for being loyal to the grandfather. Another idea that came up in the team discussion involved the belief that the grandmother had invalidated the dignity of the grandson by keeping the secret about the grandfather's violence for so many years and then revealing it to the therapist, an outsider, without first discussing it privately with the grandson.

The team dwelled in a mire of such desperate ruminations for about ten minutes, but finally, as usually occurs with systemically oriented teams, a team member stated: "there must be something positive in this situation!" Fortunately, one prejudice, if taken to the extreme, often evokes its polarity—especially in clinical teams who practise the art of flexibility and consideration of multiple views.

From this came the classically systemic prejudice: if they are still alive, something must be working for them. Can we try to look at the boy's behaviour as being useful, or in some way protective? How could this boy's seemingly aberrant behaviour be protecting other members of the family? The team suddenly woke up from the negative trance induced by the family. It found itself able to begin to create a more hopeful and resourceful story.

The team and therapist decided to build a story of family loyalty that contextualized the boy's behaviour as being a manifestation of the desire of the entire family to keep the grandfather's memory alive. The mother was empowered by recalling, in front of the whole family, stories of how she took care of her siblings during the grandfather's drunken tirades; the mother's feelings of sorrow and being broken-hearted about how the family had tried to push the memory of the grandfather out of existence were also emphasized. A therapeutic story was developed in which it was emphasized that, somehow, a situation had been created in the family in which the grandson had become the embodiment of stories about the grandfather as a way to keep his memory alive. Simultaneously, the nature of the stories seemed to keep in place the protected image of the grandmother as a long-suffering pillar of the family who had managed to keep them together under very difficult circumstances. It was suggested that there were other characteristics of grandfather that may have been worthy of re-membering—for example, he had been a carpenter who was very talented at making things with his hands, just like his grandson.

One outcome of this redescribing of the family story was for the grandson to come up with a method for helping his aunt, mother, and grandmother to handle their worries about him: any time he (the grandson) noticed them becoming nervous about the possibil-ity of his relapsing, he would reassure them by suggesting they take him for a urinalysis to assure them he had not resumed drug use.

The more resourceful story was able to be maintained in the therapy sessions and extended into the everyday life of the family. Two years after therapy ended, the adolescent continued to stay out of trouble—a senior in high school, his grades had improved, he was a star of the football team, and his use of drugs and alcohol was minimal. His relationship with his mother was greatly improved, as was the rapport between mother, grandmother, and aunt.

CHAPTER FIVE

Closing comments on the therapeutically correct

I n our culture, we have been taught to be teachers of "truth". It seems inevitable that old metaphors become reified into sanctified truths. New metaphors always play off of the old, the so-called, truths of the dominant theories of the moment.

The reader may ask just what is meant by "the therapeutically correct"? By this we mean *any* theory, hypothesis, model, or approach that claims to offer allegedly correct ways of understanding and/or changing human beings. We have an allergy to claims of correctness implied in models or orientations that pretend to offer objective answers. Some may say this view leads to nihilism, cynicism, or relativism. Yet, for us, we have been led to a search for novel ideas, excitement, and an experience of freedom, as well as responsibility and accountability. However, we are not trying to start a cult of novelty. Novelty always has to play off of the established. We agree with Alexander Soljinetzin when he said that the greatest failure of Communist Russia was the obsession with novelty and insistence on destroying the aesthetic, the rich Russian history and culture.

We see a similar naive infatuation with the alleged "new" in the field of family therapy, particularly in the rhetoric emerging in the work of some of the so-called post-modern approaches. We have to confess that it is difficult to avoid falling into the temptation of trying teach something "real" to someone. But we have no interest in evangelizing anyone. We hope we have succeeded in making this book enjoyable to read, rather than a prescription for a new orthodoxy. We also hope to have provoked the readers into realizing that they are accountable for the prejudices they allow themselves to be organized around, and for what they do.

And so, dear reader, are you prepared—rather are we prepared—to give up the reassuring safety of some of the tried and true ideological truths that have become useless in their literalness? These truths have been absolutely necessary to the creation of the family therapy movement during the past forty years. Each of these truths has been associated with very powerful leaders who, in turn, have enjoyed idolization for these important insights. Have we reached a position where we are ready to dare to question the unquestionable—even at risk of deconstructing the entire family therapy movement? We believe the field is ready for this kind of leap into the uncertainty of the future. Or, to be less grandiose, we, personally, are enthusiastically ready to make this kind of leap.

The last family therapist

conversation in the year 2016 . . .

Joe: *He awoke at the regular time to a muggy, July morning, in New Orleans. Ever since his wife and 12-year-old son left him, he started each day with four ounces of Virginia Gentleman, a fine, but inexpensive Bourbon whiskey. The whiskey helped him ease into the day and relaxed him for his first therapy appointment.*

Bob: *After a quick shower and shave, he rushed out of the front door and stepped off the curb to cross Royal Street. He awoke to the vision of a nurse leaning over him to check his vital signs. When he asked what was happening she told him he was in the hospital after having been run over by one of those ridiculous tourist horse-drawn carriages. You know, the ones you see all over the French Quarter all the time, except for when you want one.*

Harry: Bob and Joe, I don't like the story you started here. It is too tragic, too pessimistic. Give me a break, it looks like you are talking about me. Let me start the story again. *He awoke at the regular time to a muggy, July morning, in New*

Orleans. Ever since his wife and 12-year-old son decided to stay with him, after twelve wild years of marital difficulties, he started each day with a magnificent breakfast of eggs benedict with his family. After a quick shower and shave, he rushed out of the door while his son and wife were still eating. He stepped off the curb and crossed Royal Street to catch a cab to Queen Street, where an audience of 125 people were waiting to hear him give a workshop on Louisiana Eating Disorders. He awoke to the vision of a nurse leaning over him to check his vital signs. When he asked what was happening she told him he was in the hospital after having been run over by one of those ridiculous tourist horse-drawn carriages. You know, the ones you see all over the French Quarter all the time, except for when you want one.

Joe: Wait one minute while I get a drink.

Bob: Bring two glasses, Joe.

Joe: Back to the story. I have an idea, guys. *He was almost asleep, and he had a vision of a beautiful Geisha moving very slowly above him. But the chair was hard and uncomfortable. He slowly opened his eyes to see an older man lecturing in the hall about structural family therapy. He had always taken pleasure in being able to sleep through lectures, but for some reason today the man's annoying voice kept intervening with his obsessive dreams about the beautiful Japanese girl.*

Bob: What is this? I thought we were telling a story about the last family therapist, and besides I like blondes. So, lets make her a blond, not a Japanese girl. Okay, now, lets get on with the story. *He had always been able to sleep through such boring repetitions of the same old stories about boundaries and all that kind of crap, but now this annoying old man's voice prevented him from doing so. He tried to perk up and listen, hoping something new might accidentally be said in this dreary repeat of allegedly profound ideas, whereupon he dosed off, back to his dream of the beautiful girl.* That's enough from me for now—Joe, pass the bottle.

Harry: *The therapist wakes up after four days of deep coma, feeling very happy to still be alive and in one piece. There is a disturbing voice coming from a speaker which is hardly audible, and after ten minutes of blissful feelings of rest, a terrible suspicion comes to his mind. The almost inaudible voice is Minuchin's. But the voice is very difficult to understand, and the doubt creeps in that it may be Michael White's voice, or perhaps Karl Tomm, or even Virginia Satir. A sense of relief comes to the therapist when he settles down to the idea that it is the imperceptible voice of Tom Andersen, a very reassuring voice that gives some hope for the future.*

Joe: Give me a second. I want to go on with the story but I have to say that we are a pitiful lot here. We have become too obsessed with family therapy. We gave the field more importance than it deserves in our life. However, I have no other skills in the marketplace. Back to the story. *He didn't know whether he should accept the invitation or not. After all, it was one of his former clients who had invited him and his family to a birthday celebration at the New Orleans Country Club in mid January. He had to take a piss, so he left the ballroom and he wandered out to the huge, empty swimming pool. He climbed up the ladder of the high diving board. He had been a great athlete in his youth, as well as a daredevil. He walked to the end of the diving board, unzipped his pants slowly, and pissed into the empty swimming pool, then slowly walked backwards off the diving board. He thought about the last time he had some fun. The last time he had been able to stay awake for an entire family session.*

Bob: *But no, that was Carl Whitaker. When is this nightmare going to end. I'm a family therapist—I know something about how to help people, I'm just afraid because that last malpractice suit nearly broke me. I told that father to set some limits with his kid, not to lock him in the closet for six months. Christ, things were so much simpler back when Milton Erickson could instruct a mother to sit on her kid and not be afraid she would hurt him. Maybe it is time for me to go back to simpler counselling moves. That's it. I'll just start asking people "How did that make you feel", and avoid imposing my thoughts on them.*

Harry: *The last therapist woke up from the coma and discovered that the sky was clear, full of stars and absolutely beautiful. He could not figure out how many days, months, or years he had been absent from the scene. He had a frightening feeling that perhaps so much time had gone by that family therapy was totally obsolete. He thought he was really the last family therapist. He had a duty and responsibility to represent an historical witness to this magnificent movement that had happened in the past, but he could not figure out how far back this past was. So, he decided to set out to create a monument that would make people remember the history of family therapy before it died. The moment he sat up to begin, a dizziness overcame him.*

Joe: I am beginning to like this story—let me continue with it. *Later that afternoon, a tall thin man wearing an extremely baggy and rumpled suit entered his hospital room. He reeked of Old Spice aftershave and the smell was comforting. It reminded him of the many gifts from his wife. The man identified himself as the hospital chaplain and asked a very familiar question. One that he had asked a million times in his life: How are you feeling today Dr. Lance? The question was so common he found it extremely disorienting, however, he had decided to be polite for a change, since he felt his life was in the hands of these hospital bastards. The only time I ever felt better than this, he replied, was at my wife's mother's funeral. The chaplain did not find that funny, and clutched his Bible even tighter. In his perverse way, Dr. Lance wondered what he did with that Bible when he had to take a dump. But he remembered—he was trying to be polite today.*

Bob: *So he asked the chaplain to pass the bedpan, which he felt was the most polite indirect way to invite him to leave. The last family therapist began to review his life experiences. It all started off in such an exciting way. He was part of the cutting-edge field of family therapy. We were all so certain we knew so much more about context, and relationships and all that. Much smarter than those psychoanalysts. Then it began to unravel. It was almost like someone reached down and removed the cornerstone, and the whole fiction of certainty about family structure, rules, systems, homeostasis (was that Don Jackson?) were no longer being taken seriously. What in the hell is happening here? The half-life of an idea is not half as long as it used to be. But then, I'm not even sure I'm awake because each time I try* to sit up I either get dizzy or that preacher comes back to visit. So I think I'll just drift off and try to get back into that dream about that girl.

Harry: The last family therapist suddenly became very anxious. He thought he was supposed to be the last family therapist. Instead, family therapy meetings, conferences, workshops kept going on. When he accepted the definition of the last family therapist he had a glimmer of hope that the whole thing would end and an entire new life would open up for him. Instead nothing happened. Conferences, local, regional, state, national, international, global, mega-galactic, kept popping up which the last family therapist could not attend. So the last hope of the last family therapist began to fade away. After he contributed books on irreverence and prejudice, he was hoping for a respite, but he could not do it. Of course, everybody accused the last family therapist of being addicted, of being a workaholic, of being a narcissistic personality. The only hope for the last family therapist was to become obsolete. Irreverence and prejudice did not help in achieving that result. Probably we need to write another book.

Bob: Shouldn't we finish this one first?

Joe: Okay—the last family therapist was finally released from the hospital on day twenty-six. He slowly walked out of the front door of the hospital, stepped onto Royal Street, and opened the door of his wife's shiny new Jaguar. He always was terrified of riding in the car with his wife who tended to play the radio excessively loud and sing along with the music. One of his favourite things to do as a child was to sleep and dream in the car while his father drove deep into the Louisiana swamp lands. He was tired, and this day the wife didn't sing. They quietly drove the steamy streets of New Orleans, and the only thought that crept into his mind was what to do with the rest of the afternoon without being able to conduct a family therapy session.

Bob: Just then he heard the screech of brakes as his wife hit a man stepping off the curb onto Royal Street. The last family therapist jumped out of the car and ran over to the man who was lying on *the ground clinging on to three family therapy books, mumbling "my God don't let me die before I discover the answer. Ask me the miracle question, there must a solution. Nobody in my family of origin has ever been hit by a car before. The light is fading, please, Dr. Bowen, tell me the answer." I'm not Dr, Bowen, I'm Dr. Lance, the last family therapist. Tell me, just who has this problem? How have you attempted to solve it? "My God, Dr. Lance I'm lying here dying in the street."*

Harry: *So, the last therapist, after all these events, is still alive and kicking. Still the last family therapist is looking to make history, to find solutions, to be relevant and make sense, to avoid ridicule, avoid misunderstanding and abuse. Looking for legitimization, but a spark of dignity still remains in him. Nobody can crush someone who has been in a coma for such a long time. So, the last family therapist began to notice the aura of respect he was developing around him. After listening to thirty years of jargon, of selling truth, selling solutions, selling hope, still something remained that maintains the dignity of the last family therapist. Perhaps the coma did it. The coma of one month, two months, seven years, did it.*

Joe: **That reminds me of a story . . .**

REFERENCES AND SELECTED BIBLIOGRAPHY

Andersen, T. (1987). The reflecting team: Dialogue and metalogue in clinical work. *Family Process, 26*: 415–428.

Anderson, H., & Goolishian, H. (1988). Human systems as linguistic systems: preliminary and evolving ideas about implications for clinical theory. *Family Process, 27*: 371–393.

Anderson, H., & Goolishian, H. (1990). Beyond cybernetics: comments on Atkinson & Heath's "Further thoughts on second-order family therapy." *Family Process, 29*: 157–163.

Atkinson, B., & Heath, A. (1991). The limits of explanation and evaluation. *Family Process, 29*: 164–167.

Bakhtin, M. (1965). *Rabelais and His World* (translated from Russian by Helene Iswolsky). Cambridge, MA: M.I.T. Press.

Bandler, R., & Grinder, J. (1979). *Frogs into Princes: Neurolinguistic Programming*. Moab, UT: Real People Press.

Bateson, G. (1951). Information and codification. In: J. Ruesch & G. Bateson, *Communication: The Social Matrix of Psychiatry* (pp. 168–211). New York: W.W. Norton.

Bateson, G. (1961). The biosocial integration of behavior in the schizophrenic family. In: N. Ackerman, F. Beatman, & S. Sherman (Eds.),

Exploring the Base for Family Therapy (pp. 116–122). New York: Family Services of America.

Bateson, G. (1970). *An Anthropologist Views the Social Scene*. [Cassette recording of a talk given at the Mental Research Institute, Palo Alto, CA, January.]

Bateson, G. (1972). *Steps to an Ecology of Mind*. New York: Jason Aronson.

Bateson, G. (1979). *Death on a Pale Horse*. [Cassette recording]. Big Sur, CA: The Esalan Institute.

Bateson, G., & Jackson, D. (1964). Some varieties of pathogenic organization. In *Disorders of Communication, Vol. 42* (pp. 270–283). Research Publications, Association for Research in Nervous & Mental Disease.

Bateson, G., Jackson, J., Haley, J., & Weakland, J. (1956). Toward a theory of Schizophrenia. *Behavioral Science, 1*: 251–264.

Berger, M. (1978). *Beyond the Double Bind*. New York: Brunner/Mazel.

Boscolo, L., Cecchin, G., Hoffman, L., & Penn, P. (1987). *Milan Systemic Therapy*. New York: Basic Books.

Cecchin, G. (1987). Hypothesizing, and circularity, and neutrality revisited: an invitation to curiosity. *Family Process, 26*: 405–413.

Cecchin, G., Lane, G., & Ray, W. (1991). Vow strategischen vorgehen zur nicht intervention. *Famlian Dynamik,* 3–18.

Cecchin, G., Lane, G., & Ray, W. (1992). *Irreverence: A Strategy for Therapists' Survival*. London: Karnac Books.

Cecchin, G., Lane, G., & Ray, W. (1993). From strategizing to nonintervention: toward irreverence in systemic practice. *Journal of Marital & Family Therapy, 19* (2): 125–136.

de Shazer, S. (1982). *Patterns of Brief Family Therapy*. New York: Guilford Press.

Fisch, R., Weakland, J., Watzlawick, P, & Bodin, A. (1972). On unbecoming family therapists. In A. Ferber & A. Mendelson (Eds.), *The Book of Family Therapy*. New York: Brunner/Mazel.

Gadamer, H. (1987). *Philosohical Hermeneutics*. Berkeley, CA: University of Chicago Press.

Gergen, K. (1991). *The Saturated Self*. New York: Basic Books.

Goldner, V. (1988). Generation and gender: normative and covert hierarchies. *Family Process, 27*: 17–31.

Haley, J. (1959). An interactional description of schizophrenia. *Psychiatry, 22*: 321–332.

Haley, J. (1973). *Uncommon Therapy: The Psychiatric Techniques of Milton H. Erickson, M.D.* New York: W.W. Norton.

Haley, J. (1976). *Problem Solving Therapy.* San Francisco, CA: Jossey-Bass.

Hoffman, L. (1986). Beyond power and control: toward a second-order cybernetics. *Family Systems Medicine,* 4: 381–396. [Also in *Exchanging Voices.* London: Karnac Books, 1993.]

Jackson, D. (1957a). A note on the importance of trauma in the genesis of schizophrenia. *Psychiatry, 20* (2): 181–184.

Jackson, D. (1957b). The question of family homeostasis. *The Psychiatric Quarterly Supplement, 31* (part 1): 79–90.

Jackson, D. (1958). Guilt and the control of pleasure in schizoid personalities. *The British Journal of Medical Psychology, 31* (part 2): 124–130.

Jackson, D. (1960). A critique of the literature on the genetics of schizophrenia. In D. Jackson (ed.), *The Etiology of Schizophrenia* (pp. 37–87). New York: Basic Books.

Jackson, D. (1964a). *Myths of Madness: New Facts for Old Fallacies.* New York: MacMillan.

Jackson, D. (1964b). Schizophrenia: an adaptation to a socially pathogenic context. *Issues in Current Medical Practice, 1* (8): 2–7.

Jackson, D. (1965a). Family rules: marital quid pro quo. *Archives of General Psychiatry, 12:* 589–594.

Jackson, D. (1965b). The study of the family. *Family Process, 4* (1): 1–20.

Jackson, D. (1967a). Pain is a prerogative. *Medical Opinion & Review, 3* (11): 110–114.

Jackson, D. (1967b). Schizophrenia: the nosological nexus. In: *Excerpta Medica International Congress, The Origins of Schizophrenia. The Proceedings of the First International Conference, 151* (pp. 111–120). Rochester, NY.

Jackson, D. (1967c). The fear of change. *Medical Opinion & Review, 3* (3): 34–41.

Jackson, D. (1967d). The individual and the larger context. *Family Process, 6* (2): 139–154.

Jackson, D. (1967e). The myth of normality. *Medical Opinion & Review, 3* (5): 28–33.

Jackson, D., & Watzlawick, P. (1963). The acute psychosis as a manifestation of growth experience. *Psychiatric Research Reports, 16* (May): 83–94.

Jackson, D., & Weakland, J. (1959). Schizophrenic symptoms and family interaction. *A.M.A. Archives of General Psychiatry* (Dec.): 618–621.

Jackson, D., & Weakland, J. (1961). Conjoint family therapy: some considerations on theory, technique, and results. *Psychiatry, 24* (suppl. #2): 30–45.

Keeney, B. (1982). Not pragmatic, not aesthetic. *Family Process, 21:* 429–434.

Keeney, B. (1983). *Aesthetics of Change.* New York: Guilford Press.

Keeney, B., & Ray, W. (1992). Kicking research in the ass: provocation contributing to reform. *American Family Therapy Association News Journal* (Spring): 68–69.

Keeney, B., & Sprenkle, D. (1982). Ecosystemic epistemology: critical implications for the aesthetics and pragmatics of family therapy. *Family Process, 21:* 1–18.

Laing, R. (1970). *Knots.* New York: Vintage.

Laing, R. (1971). *The Politics of the Family.* New York: Pantheon.

Laing, R. (1981). *Wisdom, Madness and Folly.* New York: McGraw-Hill.

Lane, G., & Russell, T. (1987). Neutrality vs. social control: systemic approach to violent couples. *Family Therapy Networker, 11* (3): 52–56.

Lane, G., & Schneider, A. (1990). A therapeutic ritual of respect. *Zeitschrift fur Systemische Therapie, 8:* 103–108.

Maturana, H., & Varela, F. (1980). *Autopoiesis and Cognition: The Realization of the Living.* Dordrecht, Netherlands: D. Reidl.

Minuchin, S. (1990). Comments made during a presentation by J. Griffith, M. Elliott-Griffith, & T. Andersen, *Systemic Therapy with Mind/Body Problems.* AAMFT annual meeting, Washington, DC, October 6.

Palazzoli, M., Boscolo, L., Cecchin, G., & Prata, G. (1978). *Paradox and Counterparadox.* New York: Jason Aronson.

Palazzoli, M., Boscolo, L., Cecchin, G., & Prata, G. (1980). Hypothesizing–circularity–neutrality: three guidelines for the conductor of the interview. *Family Process, 19* (1): 3–11.

Ray, W. (1992). Our future in the past: lessons from Don Jackson for the treatment of hospitalized adolescents. *Family Therapy, 19* (1): 61–71.

Ray, W., & Keeney, B. (1993). *Resource-Focused Therapy.* London: Karnac Books.

Ray, W., Keeney, B., Parker, K., & Pascal, D. (1992). The invisible wall: a method for breaking a relational impasse. *Journal of the Louisiana Counseling Association, 3* (1, Spring): 32–34.

Rorty, R. (1989). *Contingency, Irony, and Solidarity*. Cambridge, MA: Cambridge University Press.

Rorty, R. (1991). *Objectivity, Relativism, and Truth: Philosophical Papers, Vol. 1.* Cambridge, MA: Cambridge University Press.

Sluzki, C., & Ransom, D. (1976). *Double Bind: The Foundation of the Communicational Approach to the Family.* New York: Grune & Stratton.

Sullivan, H. (1953). *The Collected Works of Harry Stack Sullivan.* New York: W.W. Norton.

Szasz, T. (1970). *The Manufacture of Madness.* New York: Harper.

Szasz, T. (1980). *Sex by Prescription.* New York: Penguin Books.

Tannenbaum, F. (1938). The dramatization of evil. In: *Crime and the Community.* New York: Columbia University Press.

von Foerster, H. (1981). *Observing Systems.* Seaside, CA: Intersystems Publications.

Watzlawick, P., Beavin, J., & Jackson, D. (1967). *Pragmatics of Human Communication: A Study of Interactional Patterns, Pathologies and Paradoxes.* New York: W.W. Norton.

Weakland, J., Fisch, R., Watzlawick, P., & Bodin, A. (1974). Brief therapy: focused problem resolution. *Family Process, 13*: 141–168.

Weakland, J., & Ray, W. (Eds.) (in press). *Propagations: Samples of M.R.I. Influence over 30 Years.* New York: Haworth Press.

Whitaker, C. (1976). The hindrance of theory in clinical work. In P. Guerin (Ed.), *Family Therapy: Theory and Practice.* New York: Gardner.

White, M. (1989). *Selected Papers.* Adelaide, Australia: Dulwich Centre Publications.

INDEX

ABOUT THE AUTHORS

Gianfranco Cecchin, M.D., is co-founder of Milan Systemic Therapy, one of the most influential family therapy models practiced today. Co-Director of the Centro Milenese Di Terapia Della Famiglia, Milan, Italy. World renowned for his pioneering work in family therapy, he is author and co-author of numerous journal articles and books in the field of marriage and family therapy.

Gerry Lane, M.S.W., is in private practice and is Director of Family Therapy at Hillside Hospital, in Atlanta, Georgia. Author of a number of journal articles and book chapters, he has presented workshops throughout Europe and the United States. He has gained wide recognition for his pioneering use of cybernetic and systemic orientation in research and clinical practice with couples' violence. In recent years he has devoted much of his time to the use of the systemic orientation in psychiatric and other institutional settings.

Wendel A. Ray, Ph.D., is a Research Associate and Director of the Don D. Jackson Archive at the Mental Research Institute, Palo Alto, California. He is an Associate Professor of Marriage and Family Therapy at Northeast Louisiana University in Monroe, Louisiana, and has a private practice. Author or co-author of numerous articles, and books, he has presented workshops on interactional therapy across the United States.

Learning Resources Centre